To Become Somebody

To Become Somebody

Growing Up Against the Grain of Society

John B. Simon

FOREWORD BY ROBERT COLES

Houghton Mifflin Company Boston 1982

Library of Congress Cataloging in Publication Data

Simon, John B.
  To become somebody.

    1. Simon, John B.   2. Teachers —New York (N.Y.) — Biography.
3. Problem children — Education — New York (N.Y.)   I. Title.
LA2317.S615A34   373.11′0092′4 [B] 81-13328
ISBN 0-395-32052-6   AACR2

To the enduring memory of . . .

S. Budd Simon, my father, who taught me
everything I needed to learn about
the immense power of positive role models.

Chuck Gamper, who believed in and supported
my work when I most needed help and
encouragement.

Esther Raushenbush, whose understanding
of the issues I wanted to address
helped shape and strengthen this book.

Tyrone "BooBoo" Holland, whose untimely
death fixed in my mind forever
the waste represented by every child denied
the opportunity to develop
his or her full potential.

I knew that what was sport for others was life or death for me. Therefore, I had to make it a matter of life or death for them. Not many people are prepared to go so far, at least not without the sanction of a uniform. But this absolutely single-minded and terrified ruthlessness was masked by my obvious vulnerability, my paradoxical and very real helplessness, and it covered my terrible need to lie down, to breathe deep, to weep long and loud, to be held in human arms, almost any human arms, to hide my face in any human breast, to tell it all, to let it out, to be brought into the world, and, out of human affection, to be born again.

JAMES BALDWIN,
Tell Me How Long the Train's Been Gone

Acknowledgments

Five years after I began working with youngsters in trouble on Manhattan's Upper West Side, funding for the tiny alternative public school program I had started suddenly dried up. Faced with the prospect of watching the program die and my students return to overcrowded classrooms where their complex and urgent needs could not possibly be met, I began casting about for other ways to fund my work. A day-care advocate, Bob Gangi, with whom I worked closely for several years, had joined the John Hay Whitney Foundation as a program officer. Bob agreed to explore the possibility of a grant for me but warned that the foundation did not fund direct service programs.

In the fall of 1975 the John Hay Whitney Foundation awarded me a grant to write a book about my experience working with youngsters on the margins of society. Without the foundation's timely and generous support, I would probably neither have written this book nor been able to continue my work. The views expressed on these pages are my own, however, and are not intended to represent those of the foundation.

I want to thank Bob, who helped me secure the grant, and Arch Gillies, then president of the foundation, who took a lively interest in the project and introduced me to Esther Raushenbush. Esther, for many years the president of Sarah Lawrence

College, convinced me of the importance of trying to publish my manuscript and guided me in the complex task of shaping my thoughts and experiences into a book.

I am especially grateful to Anita McClellan of Houghton Mifflin, who has exercised a compelling mixture of firmness and sensitivity in editing this book. I would also like to acknowledge Millie Hawk Daniel's editorial assistance on an earlier draft. Without the expert advice and unflagging encouragement of my friend and agent, Michael Washburn, the manuscript might still be collecting dust on a shelf.

I wish to thank the following friends for their close reading and criticism of various draft versions: Henry Adam, Tom Brown, Ted Curry, David Hackett, Betty Lorwin, Jack Mollahan, Frank Munoz, George Orio, Tom Pendleton, Arthur Powell, Jr., Peter Sauer, Frank Schwartz, and Luther Seabrook. In addition I wish to express my appreciation to Beatrice Gross, Nat Hentoff, and Herb Kohl for their valuable comments.

I owe the most, however, to the many dedicated DOME Project staff members who have worked so long and hard to make our program a success. I cannot name them all, but I would be remiss if I failed to mention those who specifically helped ease the burden of my responsibilities so I could devote the time necessary to finishing this book: Beverly Arnold, Tom Brown, Ted Curry, Bob Ellis, Linda Garcia, Miriam Llanes, Betty Lorwin, Frank Munoz, Tom Pendleton, Arthur Powell, Jr., Edwin Scott, Chris Sugarman, Shigemi Takagi, and Omar Vargas. As director of the program, I invariably get the credit for what they and the rest of the staff have accomplished. Yet without the mutual support and respect that have made our staff such an outstanding group to work with, none of us would have achieved anything worth writing about.

I wish to convey very special thanks to the members of my immediate family, who have had to put up with my overextended schedule, working vacations, and the testiness that comes from too little play. My mother, Constance "Bunny"

Simon, has always been my greatest booster. My wife, Hannele, who manages to give so much while receiving so little, has made it possible for me to work and write and still have a rich and sustaining family life. My children, Mikko and Elina, who have instructed me not to write any more books, have been a source of tremendous joy and inspiration.

Finally, I want to acknowledge the invaluable contribution of the many youngsters and parents who spent hundreds of hours working with me on the book during the past six years. Their frankness and eloquence about delicate matters of great personal concern have touched me deeply as I hope they will touch the reader. The book is theirs as much as it is mine, and I hope they will continue to make their voices heard at every opportunity.

Contents

Contents

Foreword

by Robert Coles

There is, of course, an ironic side to this book's subtitle. John Simon wants to emphasize the various necessary and important battles that must be waged on behalf of terribly hurt children — battles with bureaucrats, with welfare workers and teachers and principals themselves overwhelmed by the enormity of human pain and its consequences set before them in the course of their work. But now there is an additional struggle millions of individuals have to wage — because these are not the most encouraging times for ghetto families, not to mention such idealistic and energetic people as Simon, who work so hard and long on behalf of the poor, the vulnerable, the desperately needy.

Yet, one suspects, Simon isn't going to succumb to hand-wringing. Nor will he trim his sails, either psychologically or by way of conviction. He tells us about some fellow American citizens — children born unlucky, to say the least. He reminds us that no gene compels a boy or girl to be sad, frightened, surly, rebellious; to become drunk habitually; to play hooky; to get high (or low, very low) on one or another drug; to rob and cheat and lie; to turn violent. He reminds us that the boys and girls society describes as "culturally disadvantaged," "culturally deprived," and of "marginal socioeconomic background," and

members of this or that "racial minority," are indeed in trouble
— lots of trouble. He tells us not only about "them," but ourselves as well, since many of us are not exactly rushing to figure
out how to provide more justice in this nation.

He is right to direct our attention to his young friends, with
whom he works so persistently and imaginatively, sometimes
with success, often with failure the unhappy result. But we must
not overlook him, the one who had a happy life, who grew up
in comfortable circumstances, who went to Hamilton College
and to England's finest universities. If we are going to ask questions about the children he brings to us in these pages —
Why this outcome here? Why that turn of events there? —
we had best not forget to inquire in a similar vein of the author
and his wife. They need not, after all, live where and as they do.
Whence their courage and uncommon decency? Whence their
ability to avoid a serious occupational hazard, one may call it,
often found in those who cross in earnest various railroad
tracks, in hopes not only of seeing "the other half," but, by God,
linking arms with it politically? I refer to a self-righteousness,
a self-serving rancor, an accusatory edginess — evidence, I fear,
of the exhaustion that afflicts not only down-and-out people,
but those who adopt their circumstances.

This is a gentle, self-scrutinizing, even self-critical book. It
is not, however, without its strong-minded passages and
thoroughly tough message. John Simon and those who have
worked alongside him have, yet again, shown us that what we
do, so to speak, we can (at least to a distinctly significant degree)
also undo. Put differently, we begin to see that The DOME
Project became, for certain youths, the beginning of a new life.
When boys and girls who have *learned,* after all, to be fearful,
anxious, dispirited, aimless, mean and truculent, and nasty to an
extreme find themselves in the daily presence of truly good and
thoughtful individuals, ready and willing to comprehend what
has happened in the past, and work with enthusiasm and generosity in the present, with a strong hope that a different future

will result — then, over and over again, those youngsters will take heed. More than that, commonly: They will begin to change their ways — discard some, at least some, of the grinding doubts, the awful suspicions; instead, take the risk of a smile, an effort with a book, an ear that listens and responds in good faith.

These days, we are quick, many of us, to write off entire communities of vulnerable people, or give them our faddish lectures: Shape up — or ship out. To be sure, some ghetto children, as Simon reminds us, seem hopelessly incorrigible. They are destined for prison, and no one, not even our Ned O'Gormans and John Simons, seems likely to interrupt a trajectory of relentless criminal involvement. But there are crimes and crimes, as the saying goes. For any number of us anger and disgust are readily forthcoming when the children described in this book end up being discussed — whereas some others also mentioned in this book may not receive the same response. I have in mind the owners of the so-called welfare hotels, or in general, the slum landlords of New York City and other cities too; or the public officials who are often in collusion with such individuals; or the lawyers and accountants who arrange the various deals that end up, once in a while, as front-page stories, as Simon reminds us. Who calls such people "culturally deprived," not to mention crooks, thieves, liars — social monsters?

I know from my own work in Boston's ghettos that plenty of youths are going to end up spending most of their lives in jail — and should. Simon is not out to be sentimental. He wants, as he puts it, to give some of his young friends a "kick in the behind." They need, he knows, discipline, controls, a long skeptical look, a fiercely determined as well as open mind. But in Boston's ghettos I have seen, as he has in New York, an assortment of hustlers who rarely get the public notice our drug dealers and robbers do — yet they hire arsonists, rake in all kinds of illegal funds, put in jeopardy — every single day

— hundreds and hundreds of lives. They live in the suburbs. They are frequently white. They are so-called professional men, businessmen. Let us think of them too as we build more and more prisons and mobilize our contemporary political rhetoric.

Most of all, though, let us think, now and then, of the children who appear in the pages to follow, of their hopes and possibilities as well as their all too obvious flaws; and let us not forget what is so valuable and fine about ourselves, to be found in such lives as John Simon's, in such efforts as The DOME Project. The author of this book knows, out of his life, what Erik H. Erikson told us never to forget, that without "judicious indignation" a "cure is but a straw in the wind of history." John Simon's life would have been described in an earlier age as redemptive — the life of a healer, of a moral witness. It is no big news that there are swings to history, and one hopes and prays that soon (sooner than some say) Simon will not have to move quite so energetically "against the grain" — because more of us, all over, for our *own* (moral) sakes, will be anxious to locate ourselves on his side, as his spiritual kin.

Introduction

This book is about young people in trouble . . . with the law, with school authorities, with their parents, and with themselves. As a school teacher and youth program director on Manhattan's Upper West Side, I have spent the past eleven years trying to help such youngsters turn their lives around. Some of them, scarred by childhoods of incredible pain and deprivation, have been unable to respond. A few are now in jail or dead, while others are still on the street, taking out their anger on a frightened and uncomprehending citizenry.

The majority of youngsters with whom I have worked, however, are neither violent nor bitter. They are just as confused and frightened as the people who cross the street to avoid them or hurriedly leave an empty elevator when they enter. These young people often respond to offers of help, and many of them have not only been able to redirect their lives but have come back to assist with the next generation of youngsters in trouble.

Most of the youngsters I work with are black or Hispanic and come from low-income families which, in many cases, are headed by single parents. In some respects I find them remarkably like the white youngsters I grew up with in the small suburban village of Pleasantville, New York. Yet the circumstances of their lives are often strikingly different in ways that I can often recognize but don't always understand.

I came to New York City and to youth work in 1970, well aware that I did not know all the answers. After eleven years I have come to realize I still don't know many of the questions. Perhaps I could have saved myself a lot of anguish if, as a child, I had listened more carefully to the words of my wise and gentle Uncle Isaiah, on whose knee I loved to sit while he talked about the great Jewish scholars of ages past. I especially remember one conversation he had with a friend from the old country about a rabbi who had what my uncle kept referring to as a Talmudic mind.*

"Uncle Isaiah," I recall interrupting, knowing I risked a scolding if my question displeased him but that I might be rewarded with a delightful story if I caught him in the right mood, "what's a Talmudic mind?"

"My son," replied Uncle Isaiah, gently lowering his gaze to meet mine, "there is no way to explain to you what is a Talmudic mind. That you must acquire from years of study, discipline, and experience."

"Please try," I begged. "Please."

Uncle Isaiah smiled kindly at me as if to say, "You will see," and then, with a sigh that seemed to take him back to his own distant childhood, he proceeded in his most avuncular and learned tone. "All right. Two men come down the same chimney. One comes down clean and the other comes down dirty. Which one goes to wash?"

"The dirty one, of course," I answered, knowing full well that none of his riddles was so simply solved but finding no way to avoid giving the answer he wanted.

"Ah," intoned my uncle piously, "if you had a Talmudic mind, you would realize that the clean one would look at the dirty one, see he needs a wash, and assume the same was true

*The *Talmud*, written down in the sixth century but covering five to ten centuries of commentary, is the second most sacred set of Jewish writings. It consists of the reports of discussions of the rabbis, including legal decisions, ethics, and other matters of importance.

for himself, while the dirty one would look at the clean one and think that he also was clean. Therefore the clean one would go to wash."

"I see," I told my uncle, greatly impressed with his logic.

"No you don't," said Uncle Isaiah. "I will show you. Two men come down the same chimney. One comes down clean and the other comes down dirty. Which one goes to wash?"

"But you just told me the clean one goes to wash," I complained.

"If you had a Talmudic mind," continued my uncle, "you would know that the dirty one sees the clean one going to wash and asks, 'Where are you going?' His companion answers, 'I see you are dirty, so I am going to wash.' 'But you are clean,' replies the first man. 'You don't need to wash. If what you say is correct, only I need to wash,' and so it is the dirty one who goes to clean himself."

"Now I understand," I said, laughing self-consciously at my childish ignorance.

But once again Uncle Isaiah shook his head. "Still you understand nothing. Two men come down the same chimney. One comes down clean and the other comes down dirty. Which one goes to wash?"

"But Uncle Isaiah," I protested, "you've already shown that the dirty one will go to wash."

"My son," Uncle Isaiah replied, "perhaps now you will begin to understand why I cannot show you that which you are not yet able to see. If you had a Talmudic mind you would not try to answer my question directly but would ask yourself instead, *'How can two men come down the same chimney and one come down clean while the other comes down dirty?'* "

The reader won't need a Talmudic mind to appreciate this book, but those who can suspend for a while their assumptions about the youngsters who appear in its pages stand to derive the greatest benefit from it. While simple characterizations may be seductive, time often proves them insubstantial. We do ourselves, as well as these young people, an injustice by tarring them all with the same brush the media have used to portray the most intransigent and frightening among them.

I have spent hundreds of hours taping interviews with young people and their parents in an attempt to capture their voices and stories accurately. I have found it necessary, however, to change not only their names but enough of the circumstances of their lives to protect their identities. In certain cases, I have taken the liberty to combine quotations, descriptions, or incidents from the lives of two or more youngsters to create a composite character. I have done so in an effort to communicate their fascinating stories without either burdening the reader with too many confusing characters or endangering the anonymity of those youngsters willing to speak honestly about matters that might prove embarrassing or damaging if traced back to them.

My intention is neither to apologize for nor condone the kinds of antisocial behavior I have worked so hard to change during eleven years of working with young people on Manhattan's Upper West Side. Rather I want to share some insights into the lives and thoughts of these youngsters with readers who have no personal contact with them and, therefore, an imperfect context in which to judge their behavior. I hope to illustrate some of the circumstances that have shaped and influenced these youngsters in a way that will reflect not only their collective problems but the diversity of their personalities, a diversity we tend to lose sight of in the prevailing characterization of the children of the urban poor as universally shiftless and destructive.

Some of the young people in this book think and act in ways most readers will find utterly foreign and disturbing; others will seem more familiar and may even remind readers of their own children or the children of neighbors and friends. We must attempt to understand both the similarities and the differences if we want to find ways to help these young people. My experience suggests that deforming circumstances characteristic of these youngsters' lives can often be compensated for or altered. I have tried to show ways, some dramatic and some tedious, in which we at The DOME Project have made it possible for a number of young people to effect those changes. In doing so I have chosen to let the youngsters and their parents speak for themselves as often as possible, so the entire experience may be seen from a perspective broader than my own.

I am not arguing that I have discovered a way to help every youngster in need. The truth of the matter is that I am still standing at the hearth watching clean and dirty youngsters pop out of the same chimney. But I don't believe ignorance should become an excuse for indifference. It is important to do what we can while we struggle to learn how to do more.

PART ONE

YOUNGSTERS IN TROUBLE

Chapter One

Lee: Nowhere to Run

The children of these disillusioned colored pioneers inherited the total lot of their parents — the disappointments, the anger. To add to their misery, they had little hope of deliverance. For where does one run to when he's already in the promised land?
CLAUDE BROWN
Manchild in the Promised Land

AT THE FIRST RING I jackknifed out of bed and groped for the phone, trying to get to the receiver before another ring awakened my children. The digital clock on the night table blinked 2:40.

"Hello?"

"Hello, John?" I recognized Lee's voice. He sounded upset and possibly high. "Will you help me?"

"What's the matter?"

"Well, I guess you could say that they caught me red-handed."

"What do you mean?" I asked, trying to clear my head.

"Robbery and assault I think they said." His voice cracked. He was definitely in bad shape. "I yoked this old guy and took his wallet and . . ."

"Don't tell me over the phone," I interrupted. "Where are you?"

"The Twentieth Precinct."

"O.K., I'll be right over. Are you O.K.?"

"Yeah, I'm all right. Please hurry. And hey, John, I'm sorry to bother you."

As I put down the receiver my wife rolled over to face me. The dim light of the street lamp revealed a familiar look of annoyance mingled with resignation.

"Who was that?" she asked.

"Lee."

"Did he hurt anybody?"

"I don't think so," I replied. "He didn't say."

"So what are you going to do?" Her tone indicated she was not so much asking a question as making a statement.

"I don't know. But I told him I would come, so I'm at least going to go over there."

"Hmmph," she grumbled as she rolled back to the other side of the bed.

Extraordinarily supportive and understanding in most situations, Hannele is constitutionally unsuited for middle-of-the-night crises. Thank goodness Lee hadn't awakened the children.

The warm spring night hung heavily over Amsterdam Avenue on New York's Upper West Side. The few working street lights were ringed with soft halos, and the lingering smell of fried pork from restaurants with exotic names like *La Loma* and *Quisqueya* mingled with fumes from diesel trucks chugging grumpily uptown.

I recognized Officer Angelini at the intake desk, seated at a typewriter, a cigarette dangling from the corner of his mouth while he pecked at the machine with one stiff finger. He had arrested another of the youngsters I worked with about a year earlier, and I had found him to be a decent man with a very professional attitude toward his work.

"Good evening, officer. You got a Lee Wilson in here?"

"Hey, Simon," he responded. "How ya doin'? He one of yours? Yeah, he's in the pen. Wanna talk to him?"

4

"If it's O.K.," I said.

"Sure. He's calmed down now. He was kinda wild when I first brought him in though." *Good thing Angelini was the one who picked him up*, I thought. Lee was probably all too ready to give some angry and frustrated cop an excuse to work him over.

Lee could now see me through the wire screen. His face brightened momentarily, then settled back into a nervous frown. He had taken off his shirt, and his thick shoulders glistened with perspiration.

"He gave me quite a chase," Angelini continued. "Guess I'm not as young as I used to be. Hey, Lee. Mr. Simon, here, wants to talk to you. If I let you out for a few minutes, you gonna behave yourself?"

"Yeah."

"Got him cold," said Angelini, without a trace of either satisfaction or hostility, as he got up to unlock the door. "I was working Riverside Park when the call came over the radio. No more'n thirty seconds later, Lee, here, comes running my way. I called to him but he tries to take off through the trees. I had to chase him about two minutes, and you can see I ain't in the best of shape for running after these young kids." He indicated a waistline that rolled gently over his wide belt. "When he started to slow down, I saw him reach inside his jacket and take out something that looked like it might be a gun. I thought, 'Oh Christ, he ain't gonna make me plug him, is he?' I yelled at him and he stopped. I told him to drop what he was holding. It turned out to be the guy's wallet. He was trying to ditch the evidence."

Lee was really stoned. I could tell as soon as Angelini let him out. Some youngsters conceal their highs pretty well. Lee's face gets puffy, his eyes bloodshot and glassy.

"Thanks for coming," Lee said.

I asked him what had happened, and he told me a long, convoluted story that started with some guy on Forty-second Street hiring him to hand out leaflets for a massage parlor and then disappearing. When Lee returned for his pay, another man at the parlor had given Lee three bucks to get rid of him and told him to come back the next day to collect the rest. Lee had then walked uptown feeling more and more out of sorts. He stopped off at a friend's house and had a few drinks, then used two of the dollars to buy a couple of joints, which he smoked while walking through Riverside Park. "The next thing I know, I was standing on Riverside Drive and I seen this old man walking by hisself and there wasn't no one else around."

"Why did you do it?" I asked.

"I don't know. I just did it. I didn't have no money. Say, will they check my school records?"

"Probably. Why?"

I could see Lee was struggling to be as clear-headed as possible. "Remember how I lied about my age to get my working papers? They say I'm eighteen, but the school knows I'm seventeen. When they find out my real age, they're gonna charge me with forgery too."

I walked over and looked at the sheet Angelini was still laboriously trying to complete. Sure enough, he had Lee down as eighteen. Lee was going to jeopardize his chance for youthful offender treatment in court because of the misguided notion that he would be prosecuted for lying about his age on his working papers!

Lee returned to the pen. I made sure Angelini got his correct age on the record and thanked him for letting Lee out to talk to me. After buying Lee some milk "to calm his stomach" and promising to call his mother first thing in the morning, I left. By the time I got back into bed it was a quarter to four.

I reached Lee's mother just before she left for work at 7:30.

"Good morning, Albertha. This is John."

"If you want Lee, he's not here. A policeman called looking for him last night, but I couldn't tell him nothing."

"I think you must have misunderstood what he was trying to tell you," I said. "Lee was arrested last night. He's going to be arraigned sometime today."

6

"Hmmmm. What'd he do?"

"He mugged an old man."

"Oh, no. Did he hurt him?"

"No," I reassured her. "Pushed him around some and scared him a lot but didn't hit him or anything."

"That's good, at least. I guess I'll have to call my boss and tell him I got to have the day off. He ain't gonna like that."

"I'll probably see you in court," I said. "He'll be in the arraignment part on the ground floor."

When I saw Lee's mother in court later in the day, she handed me a slip of paper with a name and phone number. "That policeman called back," she said. "He wants to talk to you."

I looked at the number. It was for the detective squad in the Twenty-fourth Precinct. I swallowed, hard. This couldn't possibly be about the same case.

Lee wasn't called to arraignment until night court. By then, Detective Larsen had filled me in on the details of the second case. Lee had helped burglarize a restaurant near the housing project where he lived. He had played only a minor role in the theft, but the police were convinced he had been instrumental in selling the stolen property. They would be willing to reduce charges against Lee to possession of stolen property if he would help them recover the missing goods.

I found Larsen as repulsive as Angelini was congenial. A large, flaccid man with thin hair and soft, heavy hands, he wheezed when he talked and cultivated a manner that was both conspiratorial and threatening. He boasted he already knew all he needed to know in this case except where the kids had fenced the stuff they had stolen. If Lee could help him get it back he could tie up the last loose ends, and he would see that Lee's charges were reduced to a misdemeanor. Of course, if Lee refused to cooperate, there was nothing he could do . . .

I knew Lee would never rat on his friends, but I also verified from another youngster Larsen said was involved that the police had already recovered some of the stolen property and did know just what role each of them had played in the crime. I saw no reason why Lee shouldn't return as much as he could get his hands on of the rest (which, I suspected, was still hidden in closets and drawers around the projects).

Larsen kept his word and finally arrested Lee on charges of criminal trespass, which the judge adjourned in contemplation of dismissal. At this point, however, the mugging case was still pending against him.

Four weeks later Lee had his day in court. The district attorney insisted on sticking to a charge of armed robbery, and Lee was faced with going to trial without a credible defense or pleading guilty to a very serious crime. The judge indicated he would consider Lee a youthful offender and order his record sealed if he were to plead guilty. His lawyer advised him to accept.

Outside the courtroom, Lee's composure broke down completely. "A felony!" He sobbed. Two large tears started down his cheeks, leaving jagged gray streaks that looked like scars. "Nobody told me it was no damn felony. The judge said I could've got twenty-five years."

Mrs. Wilson, Lee's mother, stood a few feet from where Lee choked out these words in a tone of mingled anger and disbelief. Her expression, frozen into a mask that revealed more than it hid, never changed; nor did she move from the spot where she waited as the lawyer and I tried to calm her son. Some parents, swollen with pain and frustration, explode in court when the humiliation becomes too great to contain. Others, like Mrs. Wilson, turn to stone. Her dark cotton dress hung in neat folds from her plump frame. Beneath her flat brown work shoes, the marble floor of the Manhattan Criminal Court building had been worn uneven by the succession of grieving wives and mothers, standing as Mrs. Wilson stood now, half listening, half absorbed in her own thoughts.

"All I had was a s-stick," Lee sputtered. "And I just yoked the guy, I didn't hit him or nothin'. That ain't no armed robbery. They tryin' to make it sound like I had a damn gun." The words were coming faster now, and the tears, keeping pace, had become tiny streams.

The lawyer, a young man with sandy hair that curled over the collar of his chestnut corduroy suit, patiently repeated to Lee what the judge had said. Lee had been granted juvenile offender status because he was still seventeen and had no prior felony convictions. With juvenile offender status, Lee's guilty plea resulted in a probationary sentence. Armed robbery could, indeed, be punishable by up to twenty-five years in prison as the judge had warned, but if Lee obeyed the terms of his probation he wouldn't have to spend any time at all behind bars. Furthermore, his record would be sealed and kept apart. Upon satisfactory completion of the probationary period, Lee's conviction would be lifted, and he would be free to swear under oath he had never been convicted of a felony.

Lee looked up at me, bewildered. "What's gonna happen to me, John?"

I excused us for a moment and walked with him down the humid, ill-lit corridor where lawyers in pinstripes and lawyers in tweeds, bearded lawyers and clean-shaven lawyers, huddled with little clusters of dark faces, the defendants indistinguishable from friends and family members, all speaking in muffled yet perceptibly urgent tones. Here and there, men sporting the flashy attire of pimps and drug dealers leaned casually against the wall, smoking. I put my arm around Lee's shoulder in a way that was meant to be reassuring, but the atmosphere in the hallway made both of us self-conscious, and reluctantly I let my arm fall back to my side.

"If you had gone to trial," I explained, "you wouldn't have had a chance. The guy you robbed would simply have pointed you out the way he did in the lineup. There's no way a guilty verdict from a jury would have resulted in as good a deal as you got from the D.A. Your lawyer was right to have you plead guilty."

"Won't that mean I'll have a record?" Lee asked anxiously.

He had spoken to me several times about wanting to join the navy, and a felony conviction would make that impossible.

"Not if you keep your nose clean from now on. Let's face it: If you're gonna keep on mugging people, it won't matter what this judge did. The next one will throw your ass in jail and swallow the key." We stopped walking, and I turned to look at him. "You've got a lot more to worry about than whether or not you'll have a record. You better start thinking very seriously about what kind of a person you want to be and what kind of life you intend to lead."

Lee's eyes were still puffy, but he had stopped crying and his voice no longer cracked when he spoke. "You don't have to worry about one thing," he said. "I ain't never coming back here. Twenty-five years? Uh-uhhhh! No way. Once I get outa here . . ."

We had turned back and were approaching the spot where Lee's mother and his lawyer waited. I nodded to the lawyer, who held his hand out to Lee.

"O.K., Lee," he said. "Mr. Simon will take you over to Probation." Urging him to listen to his mother and to me, the lawyer, still holding Lee's hand, reminded Lee of the conditions the judge had imposed and then took his leave, saying, "I don't want to see you back here again."

I didn't want to see Lee back in court again either, but I had little reason to be optimistic. I had known for some time he was headed for trouble. He had a stepfather he detested and a drug and alcohol problem he was unwilling to face. He was a good worker when he was sober, but erratic attendance had already cost him several jobs. Increasingly he was turning to street crime to support himself. Occasionally he would seek me out to discuss his problems or ask for advice, but he didn't seem to be able to follow through on anything I suggested. Mutual friends warned me he was becoming increasingly depressed and hostile, especially when he was high. Underlying my worst fears was Lee's fascination with guns, a passion I had seen evolve from the moment he had first fired a BB pistol on a camping trip to the rumored possibility that he had a .38 special in his dresser drawer.

Lee was going to hurt or perhaps even kill someone if this pattern continued, and I felt powerless to stop it. Yet I was the one he had called when he had been arrested and the one he had turned to when he needed help. Why couldn't I do something to avert what seemed like an inevitable tragedy?

In the space of a month, Lee had been to court to answer charges on two very different but serious crimes. Had he learned anything that might change his behavior? He was certainly very scared, but I had seen too many equally frightened youngsters become bolder than ever once the initial shock of the court appearance wore off. Would that happen to Lee?

For nearly four years I had worked closely with Lee, trying to find alternatives to the path that had led him to court. I had come to care deeply for him but had been unable to effect any lasting changes in his lifestyle. At seventeen he was just as confused as and infinitely more dangerous than he had been at thirteen. What had I done for him? What could I do that I hadn't tried already? What message was I communicating to him by standing at his side in court, then watching him walk out with little or no understanding of what he had just been through. He still felt no greater sense of restraint than when he mugged the elderly man without being able to offer any justification for what he had done other than that he had no money at the time and thought no one was watching.

These questions troubled me deeply as Lee, his mother, and I, having made the required appointment with the probation officer following the disposition of the mugging case, walked out the door of the criminal court building and down the steps to Centre Street. It was one of those unbearably hot, humid days, typical of midsummer but unusual for this early in the year, when Manhattan becomes a pressure cooker. My nerves were frayed from the tense morning in court, and my temples throbbed as we reached the shimmering pavement.

As we started across the street toward the subway, Lee suddenly turned and walked away from us up toward Canal Street. Mrs. Wilson and I called to him to come back and ride uptown with us, but he only shouted back, "I've caused the both of you enough trouble already." He was crying again. "Don't worry about me. I'll be all right." He turned again and started running, away from us though toward whom or what we had no idea and neither, probably, did Lee.

Chapter Two

How I Got Involved

Painfully aware of my youth, I tried to belie my twenty-one years
by acting mature and seasoned by experience. My act held up,
until one horrid day when I asked a government class what was
causing the peculiar smell that hovered in the room. A sharp-eyed
pupil pointed out that I had stepped in a pile of dog crap and had
tracked it around the room. Thus died maturity.

PAT CONROY
The Water Is Wide

FOR THE PAST ELEVEN YEARS I have spent most of my
waking hours with Lee and youngsters like him, hardly the com-
panions one would expect for a middle-class Jewish boy from
the suburbs who cried himself to sleep every night for a week
in fear and mortification at having stolen his teacher's special
piece of blackboard chalk. The tougher youngsters in my town
terrified me, and I kept as far from them as I could.

I hated New York City as a child. My unformed sensibility
could not take the crush of sights, sounds, and smells that
pressed in from all sides at once. I used to visit my grandfather
in a hotel on West Seventy-third Street that smelled like dust
and mildew. He took me to museums, movies, restaurants, and
all kinds of wonderful places, but he couldn't overcome my

aversion to the city. I would have protested loudly if anyone had suggested then that I would one day live and work within a few blocks of the creepy hotel in which my grandfather was dying.

My mother says she saw signs of my future vocation in the hours I spent tutoring a retarded classmate in elementary school, but I suspect I would have done just about anything to escape the tedium of our slow-moving classes. I certainly don't recall being particularly concerned about others as a youngster. Small, funny-looking, and insecure as I approached adolescence, I wanted only to become a good basketball player and, thereby, win recognition and popularity. The lintels of my mother's house still bear fingerprints from my imaginary exploits as I whirled from the living room to the dining room to the kitchen, snaring invisible rebounds and tapping in phantom points to win a game at the buzzer for Pleasantville High.

My father had left school in the spring of 1929 to make his fortune on the stock market. Whatever can be said of his business acumen, his sense of timing left something to be desired. When the October crash shattered his dreams and bankrupted my grandfather, my father enrolled in night school and eventually earned a high school diploma. He never went on to college, but he continued to study on his own and became an extraordinarily well-educated person.

Dad was a man of consummate fairness, the kind a son can appreciate even when he is being punished. He and Mom imbued my sister and me with a deep respect for other people and would not tolerate the slightest display of conceit or intolerance. Once at a philatelic exhibition I was examining some duck-hunting stamps that had VOID printed across them in large red letters. The guard, apparently a native of Brooklyn, stooped over my shoulder and inquired, "Youse like dem pretty boids, Sonny?" I turned and, following my own train of thought rather than responding to his question, asked him, "What does *void* mean?" Before the man could answer, Dad whisked me around the corner and made it clear in the strongest possible terms that

I was never again to make fun of someone else in that disrespectful fashion. Astonished, I could only whimper that I didn't know what I had done wrong. Later, when we both realized what had happened, we could laugh at Dad's having mistaken my question about *void* for a smart-aleck crack about the guard's pronunciation of the word *bird*, but at the time I learned that other people's shortcomings were no source of merriment in our family.

Otherwise my childhood was filled with Little League and Boy Scouts, good grades and unrequited crushes. I never threw a punch in anger, and the only place I showed signs of aggressiveness was in the classroom, where harassed teachers were forced constantly to remind me not to wave my hand in their face. Every year I got cut from the basketball team, and every time I got cut I cried.

Williams College turned me down, so I went to Hamilton College in the tiny, snowy, upstate New York hamlet of Clinton. By this time I had begun to grow, but only in one direction. I hit six feet at just under 115 pounds and had a hard time making it to class in a stiff wind. I spent my junior year in Paris, living with the first working-class family I had ever gotten to know well. It wasn't until years later, however, that I realized my trip across class lines was far more perilous and ultimately rewarding than the voyage across the Atlantic.

I came back to Hamilton in 1964 for a senior year dedicated to finding a way to return to Europe. Many of my friends were becoming deeply involved in the civil rights movement, but I was far too busy for sit-ins or marches. I had set my sights on Cambridge University, and through a series of curious circumstances and coincidences, I was offered a place there to study English literature.

I was completely enchanted by the beauty of Cambridge, the gravity of its purpose. I felt myself elevated to the level of those who had earned the right to walk the halls where Sir Isaac Newton had measured the speed of sound by timing his echo, to frequent the chambers where Wordsworth penned his early verse. Then my supervisor read my first essay and brought me down to earth with the observation that if I couldn't produce anything better than third-rate derivative rubbish I ought to pack my bags and find an institution with more charitable standards.

After two years at Cambridge, with the draft board breathing heavily down my neck, I enrolled in a doctoral program at the University of York in the beautiful old Roman city in the north of England from which New York takes its name. I planned to write a dissertation on the works of Samuel Beckett, a fortuitous choice that allowed me to spend time in Dublin reading Joyce, in Paris reading Proust and Flaubert, and in Florence and Rome reading Dante. I broadened my education by marching with metalworkers in Rome, working with the makeshift ambulance corps operating out of the Sorbonne during the 1968 May rebellion, and serving as the official campaign manager for a Zimbabwean refugee standing for Parliament in one of England's most conservative counties.

Two events in 1969 changed my life dramatically. First I read *Soul on Ice.* For two days afterward I couldn't sleep or work. Cleaver's powerful images kept racing around my skull like hornets. I read *The Autobiography of Malcolm X,* and the hornets swarmed thicker and faster. I became violently homesick, not for apple pie and hot dogs, but for a place where I could put down roots and make some kind of significant contribution.

The second event was a trip to visit a Finnish friend in Helsinki. He had offered to find me a wife if I would come to see him. To my great astonishment and good fortune, he kept his promise. Although I stayed only a week with him on my way to Moscow, I met Hannele and spent enough time with her to know I wanted to see her again. We met the following Christmas in Paris, Easter in Copenhagen, and when I returned to New York in the summer of 1970 Hannele came with me to enjoy a holiday and get to know my family.

I took a free-lance job with a CBS subsidiary that was developing learning materials for preschool children and their parents. The work was interesting enough, but I couldn't get those hornets out of my skull. A research trip to a community controlled day-care center on West Eightieth Street in Manhattan, however, provided me with the chance I was looking for. The director agreed to let Hannele, who was getting bored waiting for me to return from work each day, volunteer in one of the classrooms. I was referred to the Youth Center run by the same organization, but I didn't have time to visit it until a few days later.

It was a muggy July day when I left the office and took the IRT uptown to the Youth Center. The cool church basement where the youngsters were gathered offered a welcome contrast to the stifling streets. The program director greeted me enthusiastically but was called away to settle some sort of crisis before he had a chance to show me around.

Left to my own devices, with a reticence born of the clear sense that I had entered a world very different from any I had ever known, I backpedaled into a corner and watched. Approximately thirty black and Hispanic youngsters occupied themselves with various tasks in the single room that served as office, meeting hall, and activity space. I knew they all had to be at least fourteen to qualify for Neighborhood Youth Corps jobs, but many of them looked considerably older. I felt doubly conspicuous at being not only the sole white person in the room — a situation I had last experienced in my grandmother's kitchen in Richmond, Virginia, with the cook, maid, and chauffeur — but the only one with nothing to do.

I don't know how long I waited, my thoughts bobbing unsteadily on the waves of energy generated by the noisy groups of youngsters scattered about the room, before I noticed that a short, broad-shouldered young Puerto Rican, whose name I later learned was Jorge, was heading in my direction. Without waiting for an introduction, he thrust a sheet of paper at me and asked, "Can you help me read this?"

"Sure," I replied. "Have a seat." As one of those enthusiastically didactic people who never misses a chance to teach, I was happy to seize this opportunity to make myself useful. "Try the top line," I suggested. "I'll help you if you get stuck."

"Naw. Just read it to me. I got to know what it says," Jorge asked.

"You want me to help you," I replied. "Reading it for you won't help. I'd like to see how much you can do."

"I can't do nothin'," Jorge said.

I understood his embarrassment at being a poor reader, but I was determined to show him he didn't have to be defensive with me. I was prepared to be very patient, but I had no intention of babying him. "Come on," I urged. "I'm sure you read better than you're letting on. Lots of people have some kind of reading problem. It's nothing to be ashamed of."

"I ain't got no reading problem. I just can't read." An unmistakable tone of annoyance was creeping into Jorge's voice. "I asked you to read me the paper, that's all. Are you gonna do it or not?"

Undaunted, I made one last effort. "Just try these few words. I'm sure you can do them. Don't wor . . ."

"Look, man," Jorge exploded, "I told you I can't read. Not a page, not a word, not nothin'. If you ain't gonna help me, just say so."

"But that's impossible," I stammered. "Don't you go to school?"

"Sure, I go to school sometimes. So what? They never taught me nothin' there."

By this time, I was beginning to grasp the obvious. Jorge couldn't read at all, and my insistence was only making him angry. I sheepishly took the page and read it to him, my face flushed and my thoughts racing far from the simple instructions Jorge was listening to so intently.

I wondered then as I wonder now how a youngster can reach the age of fourteen without being able to read a word. Every child in my class in Pleasantville had learned to read, even the severely limited boy I tutored for a while. Jorge was a bright, articulate youngster. What kind of society did we live in that could completely ignore his potential?

Reading *Soul on Ice* and *The Autobiography of Malcolm X* had prompted me to think of a career in prison work, but meeting Jorge changed my mind. What sense did it make to try to rehabilitate adults if society was disabling children and speeding them toward prison faster and with greater certainty than any program could possibly rehabilitate them once they got there? I decided instead to stay on the street and work with young people before they became disheartened, embittered, and ultimately incarcerated.

Jorge was not what I would call a social deviant, although he occasionally had to pilfer food or sleep in abandoned buildings to survive. While the norms to which he responded were very different from those I had known when I was growing up in Westchester, they were often admirably suited to the circumstances with which Jorge had to cope. On a day-by-day basis, he knew how to take care of himself far better than I did at a comparable age.

Most of us, however, want more out of life than bare-bones survival. When one measured Jorge's chances for a safe, happy, and fulfilling life, his problems and limitations acquired new and more sinister dimensions. We think of a youngster who sleeps in doorways and steals an occasional apple from the neighborhood stand as a scamp and a rascal, terms loosely associated with a romantic and adventurous existence, but adults who grow old adhering to the same strategies for survival are considered derelicts and bums deserving little or no respect.

I now realize I learned far more from Jorge about myself than I did about him. To sustain even a casual relationship with such youngsters, I had to suspend assumptions and judgments as difficult to shed as old habits. I couldn't rely on previous experience to guide me but had to trust my instincts and the good will of the people with whom I worked.

Not long after my first meeting with Jorge I allowed myself

to be talked into accepting the recently vacated director's position at the Youth Center. I didn't need the job. A wiser man wouldn't have taken it. But I was twenty-six and very full of myself. Armed with nine years of university training and an appalling ignorance of the world I was about to enter, I set out to do battle against the forces of injustice.

Chapter Three

Michael: Circumstances Beyond His Control

It turned out then, that summer, that the moral barriers that I had
supposed to exist between me and the dangers of a criminal
career were so tenuous as to be nearly non-existent. I certainly
could not discover any principled reason for not becoming a
criminal, and it is not my poor, God-fearing parents who are to
be indicted for this lack but this society.

JAMES BALDWIN
The Fire Next Time

MORE THAN A THOUSAND schoolchildren followed the tiny
casket as the funeral cortege twisted through the crowded
downtown streets. Many of them carried signs asking HOW MANY
MORE MUST DIE? or promising WE WILL NEVER FORGET. By the
time the mourners began filing past City Hall, the crowd had
swelled to over five thousand, and mounted police nervously
surveyed the throng for signs of trouble. Inside the somber
limousine, Tiny's mother, Edna, sobbed quietly by my side.

EDNA: My son was dead already. Nothin' I could do would
bring him back, whether I buried him just quiet like I
wanted to or did it in a public way. I figured it couldn't hurt
him, but at first I didn't feel like *I* could go through with it.

21

And yet, I had other kids, too. If it would help someone, some other child . . .

Seven-year-old Tiny had fallen through a broken elevator door in the Vernon Hotel on West Seventy-third Street to his death fourteen floors below. Two weeks earlier we had given the management of the hotel a list of all the elevator doors that didn't work. Nothing had been done to repair them. The newspapers called Tiny's death accidental, but I felt at the time he had been murdered by bureaucratic indifference and unrestrained greed.

I was the full-time director of the Youth Center by this time. My predecessor, whom I liked and admired tremendously, had left unexpectedly, forcing the board of directors to search hurriedly for a replacement. When they offered me the program director's position and Hannele a teaching job at the day-care center, she and I didn't really have much of an opportunity to discuss our decision. Hannele had already returned to Finland, and I had to work up all the nerve I could muster for a long-distance-telephone marriage proposal. In October 1970, Hannele and I were wed in Helsinki and two weeks later found an apartment in Manhattan on West Seventy-eighth Street just two blocks from where we both would work.

My first week as director, a staff member told me about the Vernon Hotel. My initial reaction was that he had to be exaggerating the horror of the conditions he was describing. I grabbed my jacket and insisted he take me there.

My father lived in the Vernon Hotel for a few years as a young man, but he would scarcely have recognized the once-elegant residence from the cadaverous slum dwelling it had become by the autumn of 1970. Junkies defecated in the stairwells amid the uncollected garbage. Alcoholics sprawled unconscious in the lobby, where residents and visitors had to step around or over them. Men and women sold drugs, stolen merchandise, and their bodies in the neighboring streets, often bringing their customers back to their hotel rooms to consummate their tawdry business. In the midst of all this degradation and filth, an extraordinary array of ill-wiped and partially clothed children played as best they could.

Edna had not chosen this environment for her family. Burned out of her apartment in the Bronx by a fire she suspected the landlord had set, she had been moved "temporarily" into the Vernon Hotel two years earlier by the Department of Social Services. She shared a two-room suite with her elderly parents and six children aged four to fifteen.

Apologizing for the mess, Edna let my coworker and me into her two-room suite on the fourteenth floor. Although the rooms were clean, I noticed that almost everything in them seemed to be broken. Beds were propped up on milk crates or bricks, chunks of plaster hung down from the ceiling, and in place of a window a sheet of stained plywood was nailed up to keep out the biting November wind. Edna explained that her parents and the baby slept with her in the two single beds in the room where we were standing, while the other five children slept on a double and a single bed in the other room.

The narrow hall linking the two rooms held the stove. Edna showed us the scars on the legs and belly of her second youngest child, who had pulled a pan of hot grease over on herself. We saw where the bathroom ceiling had caved in over the toilet and noted that the toilet in the suite directly above hers was still leaking steadily. Edna's bathtub was full of dishes, some clean and some soaking. I noticed too that there was literally no place for the children to play except on the beds. The windows next to the bed on which they were bouncing vigorously had no protective gates to keep the children from falling out.

For these two rooms and a weekly change of linen, the city's Department of Social Services was paying the management of the Vernon Hotel the unbelievable sum of $247 per week, or nearly $1000 per month.

I want to emphasize that Edna never saw this money, nor did she derive any benefit from it. She was merely a conduit or pass-through mechanism by which money changed hands between the city and her landlord. The Vernon was only one among dozens of such hotels where absentee owners reaped windfall profits from the suffering of welfare families. Most of these buildings provided fashionable lodgings for the city's gentry at the turn of the century but had fallen upon hard times as the rising cost of labor and the difficulty of maintaining antiquated buildings cut into their profitability.

Casting about for a way to milk some additional income from these buildings before gutting them, the owners came across a city agency in urgent need of temporary shelter for displaced families. Or perhaps the city, in its desperate efforts to find furnished rooms, made the first overtures. In either case, the shoe fit perfectly. The poorest neighborhoods in the city were either collapsing or burning, and there was no available rental housing stock to absorb the displaced families.

The state limited the amount of rent the Department of Social Services could pay to house welfare families. By the time Edna's building in the Bronx caught fire, there were already more displaced people waiting for apartments than there were vacant apartments available for such families. A little-used loophole in the law, however, allowed the city to pay exceptional rents for temporary shelter on a daily basis in emergency situations. Invoking this provision, the city began filling up hotel rooms with families they could not place in apartments. The hotels charged the city a per-person/per-day rate and ran up the bill by shoehorning four or five people into a single room.

When I met Edna there were approximately five thousand people, most of them children, living in various welfare hotels scattered throughout the city. They were terrible places for anyone to live, but the children suffered the most. There was no place to play. There was no privacy. Children of every age were exposed to all kinds of vice and degradation. Many parents, having been assured they were only moving to the hotel temporarily, failed to register their children for school. But the promised apartments never materialized, and the children sat, unsmiling, and stared at nine-inch black and white TV screens whose harsh light provided their only link to the outside world.

I got to know many of these hotel children, but the one I became closest to was Michael, Edna's third and the next oldest from the tragically short-lived Tiny. Michael, in contrast to his younger brother, was tall and strong for his age. At eleven he looked fourteen and already towered over his mother. His large eyes were curious and alert, but he kept to himself more than the others and spoke only haltingly and with reluctance. Often he would get so frustrated trying to express himself he would stop in midsentence and say, "Forget it."

Michael resented living in the hotel just as he had resented the slum he had been living in before the fire. This resentment took root in him where laughter and playfulness should have been growing. Nourished by the thousand injustices he had to endure, the resentment eventually grew until it consumed much of what was good and loving in him.

MICHAEL: It was terrible living in a hotel. You were uncomfortable all the time. There was no privacy. You felt like there was no such thing as peace and never would be again.

We had these two rooms, and all nine of us had to stay in them. I was supposed to sleep on two beds with my two sisters and two brothers, but a lot of times I would just take a blanket and sleep on the floor. After a while I got used to it.

My mother wouldn't let us go out at all, so I never made any friends while we lived there. When I went to school, I don't know, I just felt out of place. I thought all the other kids looked down on me 'cause I lived in a hotel like that.

Except when we was in school, we just stayed in that room by ourselves. We had this little black and white TV. When it wasn't busted, we used to watch it all day long.

The hotel was a screwed-up place to live at. Terrible as it was, you had to stay there all the time. Go out for even a minute and somebody'd break in and steal the little bit of

25

stuff you got. It made you feel somehow less than human. When I think of that place, I think of a coffin where all of us crawled inside to wait to die.

EDNA: A lot of the people in the hotels was more or less like myself. Circumstances, whatever, put 'em there. A lot of them did worse than me. I saw ordinary people come in who left as junkies, and their children too. The hotel did it to 'em. Just movin' to a place like that make you feel bad. Then havin' to go through all them other things — the fires, the constant fightin', the rats and roaches — you already be weak so you got nothin' to fight back with.

The kids, they want to live like other kids, not be cooped up in no hotel. All my children was affected by it, but Michael, he suffer the worst. From all the problems and tension, he just drawed up into a knot. He became real quiet. He never was that way before. I watched it happen, and there wasn't nothin' I could do to stop it.

At the time I was "discovering" the Vernon Hotel, the commissioner of the Department of Social Services was calling an unprecedented meeting to bring city officials and community leaders together to find ways to provide multiple services for the hotel's beleaguered residents. A special medical team from Roosevelt Hospital, which had brought the seriousness of the health emergency to the commissioner's attention, opened the meeting with a slide show and report. In addition to the broken windows and unsafe elevators, the team chronicled findings of disease endemic in the plumbing and water supply and an infestation of rodents and vermin so severe that the entire hotel would have to be evacuated for a week or longer to permit exterminators to do a safe and effective job.

Our organization was invited to the meeting because of our proximity to the hotel and because the day-care center where Hannele worked had a reputation for innovation and excellence. The commissioner asked us to set up a day-care center in the hotel to serve the children and their families. As soon as we left the meeting, however, the director of Hannele's center pointed out to me that such a program could be used to justify the continued existence of the hotel. Our primary goal should be closing the hotel and getting those families into proper apartments.

The Youth Center, which bustled with activity during the summer, had not developed a function for itself during school hours. Thus the staff and I were free to spend most of our time not only in the Vernon but in the half dozen other welfare hotels we discovered in our immediate neighborhood. We began by organizing parents to help set up a day-care center, not in one of the hotels but in the church basement where our Youth Center was located. Whatever teenagers we could attract would be able to help with the younger children. The emergency condition seemed clearly to deserve priority over the use of our space for after-school arts and crafts.

This day-care center became the nerve center for a citywide effort to expose the scandalous conditions in welfare hotels and get the city to stop warehousing people in them. Other groups became interested, including George Wiley's National Welfare Rights Organization, which brought in professional organizers to help direct the struggle. My job was to work with the hotel families, seeking out the people who weren't too defeated to fight back and bringing them together to impress upon city officials the urgency of their plight.

Our first dramatic move was a sit-in at Department of Social Services headquarters. Seventy families went there to demand apartments and ended up staying a week. For a few days city officials worked feverishly to meet the protesters' demands. Rules and guidelines were adjusted, pressure was applied to landlords who had received tax abatements or low-interest municipal loans, and rewards were offered to anyone who could find an apartment for hard-to-place families.

The round-the-clock sit-in also brought the welfare hotel situation out into the open. The media, sensing a major story, began uncovering some interesting statistics and relationships. The *New York Times* ran an investigative series on what was now being called the welfare hotel crisis. The *Daily News* ran a front-page story about a family of twelve for whose cramped and wholly inadequate hotel quarters the city had paid $35,000 over a twelve-month period. The *Village Voice* printed an exposé entitled "Who Owns Those Hotels?" uncovering close links between the owners of some of the most offensive hotels and individuals with powerful political connections in the city. *Newsweek* ran a cover story on welfare hotels, showing that the situation, while clearly out of control in New York, also existed in other cities across the country.

The sit-in ended on a Sunday night, when acrid black smoke began billowing up from the ground floor of an otherwise unoccupied office building. The protesters, many of whom had been burned out of their homes before, lost no time in heading for the exits. I could not prove that the fire was set deliberately, but I found it curious that what seemed like a battalion of riot police appeared almost immediately to seal off the building once we were outside, while the fire department seemed to take ages to arrive from a firehouse just a few blocks away.

Despite this setback, the movement began to pick up steam. While we tried to apply pressure on New York's Housing Authority to open up public housing projects to hotel families, taxpayer anger was rising with each revelation of how much these "temporary" arrangements cost. Some Department of Social Services employees, apparently angered by what was happening, placed a welfare family in the Waldorf-Astoria for two nights and then tipped off the press. The media really had a field day with that story.

Meanwhile, an even larger group of hotel families than had engineered the previous sit-in broke into a nearly completed apartment complex on Columbus Avenue that was being built with enormous state subsidies. The families were protesting the use of government money to underwrite housing for people who could afford decent homes while poor people were being imprisoned in unsafe and unhealthy hotels at tremendous cost. The occupation lasted only a few hours, but the squatters got their point across.

Edna did not take part in the break-in. She felt it would not be safe for her children, and she didn't feel she could entrust them to anyone else in the hotel. While she was preparing dinner, her children played in the hallway. That is when Tiny fell against the defective door and down the unprotected elevator shaft.

Up to this point, the city's administration had shown little inclination or ability to resolve the welfare hotel crisis. One recommendation from City Hall had been to turn the abandoned air force base at Floyd Bennett Field in South Brooklyn into a temporary (Where had we heard that before?) camp for hotel families. Somehow the offer of deserted barracks and trailers on an isolated air strip surrounded by barbed wire didn't appeal to the families. It only served to reinforce their impression that the city did not care about them as people.

Tiny's funeral was apparently the straw that broke the city's intransigence. Shortly after the cortege of schoolchildren followed the tiny casket past the steps of City Hall, the administration announced that the worst hotels were being condemned and emptied. Housing Authority teams moved into the hotels and began processing applications and moving families into public housing projects at a rate we had been told only weeks before was impossible. Within months the worst hotels were vacant and their occupants relocated into suitable apartments.

Why couldn't — or didn't — the city move earlier? We may never know the whole story. Real-estate interests wield enormous political power in New York City, and the welfare hotel system that forced so many families to live in dangerous and degrading conditions was not, in and of itself, illegal. Yet I still cannot muster the generosity to lay the entire blame on the inadequacies of an imperfect bureaucratic system, any more than I can attribute specific wrongdoing to any public official.

At the time, however, I was in a constant rage. I drove myself to do things that astonish me when I look back on them. Those hotels were dangerous places, even for people who knew how to look after themselves. I roamed around them at all hours of the day and night, butting into other people's business, armed only with my ignorance and innocence. I think I must have been accorded the safe passage bestowed in ancient times upon the visionary insane.

I had never encountered conditions such as those I ran up against in the welfare hotels. I hope never to see their likes again, for this was not Calcutta's slums but Manhattan's West Side. Most of the hotels I worked in were only a block or two from Central Park West on one side and West End Avenue on the other. I am convinced those hotels might still be plying their awful trade if they had been located in some remote corner of Brooklyn or the Bronx, but too many rich and influential people live in our community to allow such unsavory conditions to fester right under their noses. When those people finally decided enough was enough, City Hall got the message.

Edna waited patiently for the Housing Authority to offer her an apartment, but the size of her nine-member family worked against her. There were no four-bedroom vacancies in housing projects anywhere in the city. While other families moved into permanent homes, Edna was forced to settle for another temporary apartment on an urban renewal site in our neighborhood in a building that was scheduled for demolition.

While I lost contact rather quickly with those hotel families who moved to other boroughs, I continued to work closely with those who stayed in our community. Michael continued to attend our center, and we began to realize that he had not left his problems behind when he moved out of the hotel.

MICHAEL: I never had a decent place to live in when I was young. We would just move from one slum to another. Something was always happening to keep us on the move.

If it wasn't a fire, then the building was being condemned or the landlord would abandon the place and leave us without no heat or hot water.

I used to wonder, "Why do I have to live like this?" I would go to other kids' homes and see they didn't live the way I do. They got their own room, their own things. Sometimes all nine of us be crowded in just one room. I could never understand why that had to happen to me.

I was always the biggest guy in my class, but I couldn't read or write so I always felt out of place. I couldn't catch up 'cause I was too far behind and too ashamed to admit it.

Sometimes I felt like I was being punished for something I didn't do. All I wanted was to be normal like everyone else. I never had a bike or a basketball. That might not seem so important to someone else, but to me it was terrible.

Michael had a clear sense of the difference between right and wrong, a strong work ethic he derived from his mother, and an enormous desire to please and be accepted. With all these things going for him, he stood out from his more childish peers in the Youth Center. He attracted the friendship and respect of the staff, who saw in him a youngster striving to overcome the deficits of a distorted childhood.

But there were other, darker, forces at work in Michael's personality. The frustration engendered by the gap between his intelligence on the one hand and his poor skills and difficulty in expressing himself on the other gradually turned to bitterness as he saw others moving ahead while he struggled to master basic levels of competency. Instead of plodding ahead he developed a habit of making excuses for himself. Little by little Michael began to establish a double standard, one for himself and one for the rest of the world, in direct response to his sense that the world had singled him out for unfair treatment.

Michael's size and exceptional strength only complicated matters. If he couldn't explain what he wanted, he could often simply take it. Other youngsters curried favor with him in return for protection. I don't believe Michael ever wanted it to be that way, but the role had already been defined for him by circumstances beyond his control.

The Vernon Hotel killed Michael's younger brother. A case can be made that it and the similar slums that imprisoned Michael's childhood killed a part of Michael too. They bottled him up, shoving laughter and tears so far back into his subconscious that they atrophied. Michael struggled to maintain a sense of balance between what he dreamed of and what his senses told him was real, but it was a struggle he was ill equipped to undertake alone.

I felt at the time that if our Youth Center was going to accomplish anything significant, we would have to address the kinds of difficulties that were holding Michael back. I knew I would never forget Edna's courage nor the lessons I learned in those wretched hotels, but I wondered how much value they would be in trying to help Michael deal with his anger and bitterness as he entered the difficult and unsettling period of adolescence.

Chapter Four

Isaac: Bored to Death

What accounts for such durability, such a hardy spirit against such odds? Where did [this particular child] find his strength? Is his case an exception that proves nothing? It certainly is not an unusual story.

ROBERT COLES
Children of Crisis

WELFARE HOTEL FAMILIES weren't the only residents of our community with serious housing problems. Many low-income families simply couldn't find adequate places to live. With the survival of their families at stake, some parents began to resort to extraordinary measures to secure shelter. Isaac was just eleven years old when his family broke into a tinned-up building on the West Side Urban Renewal Site and set up housekeeping.

ISAAC: I remember the night we moved like it was yesterday. We came up Ninetieth Street in a truck. Some men with crowbars had already started tearing the tin off the doors, so I jumped out and got a stick and tried to help them. I was really excited.

When we got inside, what a disappointment! Twelve dead rats in this corner . . . eight more over there . . . garbage everywhere. And boy, did it stink!

Isaac's mother, Mary, had been living in a studio apartment with her teenage daughter and Isaac, but the recent arrival of another child made it imperative for her to move. The income she earned as a maid, however, wouldn't pay for the two-bedroom apartment she needed.

MARY: Lord, I looked and looked for an apartment. I dragged that baby all over the city. The more I kept lookin', the more the kids kept growin', and still I couldn't find nothin'.

Then this friend told me about the squatters movement. She said there was these buildings the city owned but had closed up so nobody could live there. They was planning to knock them down sometime, but nobody seemed to know when. Somehow it didn't seem right to have good apartments going vacant when people couldn't find a decent place to live.

After some lively negotiations, city representatives agreed to accept rent from Mary and the other squatters who had moved in at the same time. City officials agreed to reopen several inhabitable buildings on the site and a few months later moved Michael and his mother into the apartment immediately above the one Mary and her family had chosen.

For two boys of the same age who had grown up under comparable conditions of deprivation, Isaac was remarkably different from Michael. Where Michael was tall and well-built, Isaac had a scrawny little body barely capable of holding up his enormous head. And he was the dirtiest, most raggedy boy I had ever seen. No matter how clean he was when Mary sent him out of the house, within minutes he resembled a walking dust ball.

Poverty and injustice made Michael bitter; Isaac seemed convinced that the world was his oyster. Where Michael was taciturn, Isaac wouldn't stop talking. But he didn't just run his mouth. He was smart, perceptive, curious, and often thoroughly engaging, even when he was saying things that would have sounded atrocious coming from the mouth of any other twelve-year-old.

ISAAC: The main influence in my life was the block. I couldn't wait to get up in the morning to go stealin'. I never hung out with guys my age. At nine or ten I was snatchin' purses, cuttin' school, and gettin' high. Some of the kids on the block went to school, but I didn't hang out with them. If they didn't drink or smoke, I figured they was square.

I started smokin' 'cause I saw Mom do it. I felt if she could do it, so could I. She knew I wasn't no goody-goody, but she didn't know what to do about it. She'd whip my ass when she had to, but it had to be for somethin' serious.

I always knew what was right and wrong, but I also knew how to get over on Mom. She would try to reason with me, but I was hipper than most kids. She couldn't just throw me out on the sidewalk and tell me to play hopscotch with them other little niggers.

Isaac taught me that there really is such a thing as being too smart for one's own good. He was so quick and so clever that he actually undermined his own education. He learned to deduce answers from the teacher's intonation or the shape of the question. School became a game for him in which he tried to "get over" with an absolute minimum of effort. By the time he reached junior high school, he had developed no reliable academic skills and absolutely no sense of discipline. He had an extensive vocabulary but could barely read; he could shoot craps with the slickest hustler on his block but didn't know his multiplication tables. He came to school when he felt like it, bothered to attempt his assignments only if something about them aroused his interest, and often fell asleep at his desk.

Michael reacted to his oppressive living conditions by developing a roiling anger that kept him in a constant state of agitation. Isaac, on the other hand, never seemed to let anything bother him more than momentarily. He seemed to be saying, "Well, there's nothing I can do about the way things are, so why get upset about them?" He didn't have clean clothes? He'd get used to wearing dirty ones. He'd done something wrong? So he'd get yelled at for a while. Big deal. Whoever was making the fuss would eventually get tired and leave him alone. He learned to roll with every conceivable kind of punch, becoming totally passive in the face of adversity.

Isaac's strategy proved remarkably effective. Even his mother got tired of disciplining him when he seemed to accept all forms of punishment with total equanimity. By the time he reached the age of twelve, Isaac was pretty much free to come and go as he pleased. He stayed out late or watched TV until he fell asleep, then slept through the school day. When I met him he had completely reversed normal sleeping patterns so that he was routinely awake all night and asleep when he should have been in school.

Isaac had only one problem with this remarkably passive existence. He discovered that licentiousness quickly degenerates into boredom, and boredom was the one thing Isaac could not tolerate.

ISAAC: There's nothin' to do in the street except maybe play ball, and I never cared about that. So all you got left to do is hang out.

Now hangin' out can be great when you're all in a good mood, but most people got a lot of problems. They be comin' out of their houses all gloomy and sad. When everybody's down like that, hangin' out with them just gets you all depressed. That's when you gotta get high.

No matter how many things you got on your mind, when you get high they go away. Everything seems different. You can stay in one spot, doin' nothin', but your mind'll be occupied. You're not bored, but you're not worried either.

School was even more boring than doing nothing. The only way I could take school was when I was high. I used to get high every single day I went to school. So did most of my friends. We already be high by the time we get there. And let me tell you, when you're enjoyin' a high, there's no way schoolwork can fit in.

Isaac tried everything: Carbona, glue, marijuana, pills, LSD, cocaine, and opium (which he told me was like pot only stronger). Once he passed out in the street a block from the Youth Center. We carried him inside and woke him up. When I asked him the next day what he had taken, he could only tell me he had swallowed "some brown pills." When I pressed him to tell me what they were, he admitted he didn't have the slightest idea. All he knew was that the friend who supplied them told him they would produce a good high. (They turned out to be a drug commonly used to tranquilize patients in mental hospitals.) When I raised my voice to impress upon him the stupidity of swallowing things he knew nothing about, he merely shrugged his shoulders and said he really hadn't enjoyed the brown pills so much and probably wouldn't take any more anyway, so what was I getting so upset about?

Another time Mary called for me to come quickly to her apartment. I arrived to find Isaac sprawled on top of his bed, fully clothed, covered with mud from head to toe and semicomatose. We tried everything we could think of to wake him, but when all our efforts failed, I heaved him over my shoulder, hailed a cab, and rushed him to St. Luke's Hospital, where attendants pumped an entire bottle of Valium out of his stomach.

Two days later, Isaac cheerfully explained to me that he had slipped past the doorman of a luxury apartment building on West End Avenue to go exploring. A tenant caught him upstairs and summoned the police. Afraid to be caught with a pocketful of pills but unable to hide them anywhere, he had swallowed them all. The effects didn't hit him until after the policemen finished lecturing him and sent him home, but on the way he became drowsy and began to slip and fall. He didn't remember getting home but was glad he had and apologized for all the trouble he had caused by his little adventure.

Isaac not only abused drugs, he sold them too. As he put it, "Almost everybody's a dealer in a sense, because that's the main way kids can get the money they need to buy drugs. They don't look at it like they actually sellin' it. They just be tryin' to get some for themselves." Thus Isaac, not yet a teenager, was already a practiced thief and drug dealer.

What astonished me was the almost casual way in which Isaac participated in these criminal activities. He would decide to go purse-snatching much the way my friends and I used to organize a sand-lot football game. The money they obtained, usually only a dollar or two after it was divvied up among the whole crew, was almost incidental. What they were after was excitement, something to break the grip of terminal boredom on their lives.

When I was Isaac's age, my parents always knew where I was and what I was doing. If I wasn't involved in some kind of organized activity like Boy Scouts, I was playing at a friend's house. But organized activities are few and far between in poor communities, and friends' houses are likely to be just as claustrophobic, lacking in playthings, and filled with irritable adults as home. These youngsters don't have money, so they can't pay for entertainment. Their only alternative is to seek diversion on the street.

Most working people don't spend much time on the street. When they aren't at work they are usually at home, taking care of the children and the apartment or collapsing in front of the TV set. But the pimps and prostitutes, drug dealers and sellers of stolen merchandise work on the street. They are visible day and night, flashing their bankrolls and cruising around in their long, sleek cars. They are the only members of the community with an obvious supply of surplus capital, and in the eyes of these impressionable youngsters they contrast strikingly with the adults who work long hours for small paychecks and never seem to have an extra couple of dollars for the movies.

These petty underworld figures do not appear to our youngsters as parasites or hoodlums but only as friends, neighbors,
or relatives. Children compete for the chance to run errands for
them in return for loose change. Teenagers turn to them for
loans when no one else will help out.

The pressures that lured or drove so many adults to work the
streets weigh heavily upon these younger brothers and sisters.
The quest for power, the lust for riches, the hunger for sensual
fulfillment run rampant among young people afflicted with
unrelenting boredom. Not the boredom of otherwise busy people who find themselves suddenly and temporarily with nothing
to do but the deep and abiding boredom of having nowhere to
go, nothing to do, and no prospect of that condition ever changing. The boredom of a neighborhood mired deep in unemployment. People, in an increasingly mobile society, stuck in unin-
habitable lodgings because there is no place to go. The sharp
and persistent boredom of those to whom the good life is transmitted every night, right into their own shabby living rooms, by
the TV set that sells idyllic vacations and luxury items as effectively to those with no hope of buying them as to those who may
someday enrich the advertisers. Without this boredom, drugs
and easy money might lose much of their allure.

Sometimes parents with strong moral values can help their
youngsters resist the pull of the streets. Unfortunately, Mary
provided no such anchor for her children. Too tired and beaten
down by her own struggles to keep up a running battle with her
incredibly resilient son, she gave in to his headstrong behavior.
When she noticed that Isaac was coming home high, she agreed
to let him get high at home in the hope that she could at least
keep track of what he was doing. The net effect, however, was
to convince Isaac that there were no limits he needed to respect.

In high school I drank beer on Saturday nights to prove how
grown up I was, but no one I knew ever used drugs. In fact, I
didn't even see my first marijuana joint until I was in graduate
school in Europe, which says more about my age and the rural,

conservative college I attended than it does about my morality or inclinations. In England I had the opportunity to get high when I wanted but never indulged to the point where it became regular practice. I returned to New York with a fairly hip, tolerant attitude about most kinds of drug use, but all that changed radically the day a thirteen-year-old boy named Ace began nodding out on me in an elevator in the Vernon Hotel. I didn't draw any parallels between his heroin habit and my occasional use of marijuana. I just developed a feeling of revulsion every time someone passed a joint in my presence.

Whether or not a case can be made for recreational drug use by adults, I have become an impassioned opponent of drug use by adolescents. Ace may have been an extreme example, a thirteen-year-old junkie whose life was shot before he even reached manhood. But I have seen nothing in my eleven years of working with young people to contradict my sense that getting high and growing up are divergent paths.

The transitional period from childhood to adulthood should be a time for youngsters to become vividly aware of their strengths, weaknesses, and potential for change. They must experience pain to learn how to withstand it, experience boredom as an incentive to developing inner resources, and experience frustration in order to acquire the discipline necessary to overcome it. Drugs don't solve these kinds of problems, but they obliterate the symptoms and create a false sense of well-being. Youngsters who have no physical dependency on drugs begin to rely on them for psychological and emotional support. Instead of facing and resolving problems, they habitually avoid them and use drugs to postpone the emotional consequences. Such behavior prolongs immaturity, sometimes indefinitely.

Nowhere have I seen the early symptoms of this tragic pattern more clearly than in Isaac. His answer to every challenge was, "Oh, I could do it if I wanted to," but somehow he never got around to making good on that boast. When time came to put up or shut up, he usually shrugged his shoulders and backed off. "I only said I could do it. That don't mean I'm necessarily gonna do it right now. Don't worry, I'll get around to it when I'm ready."

Isaac reminded me of Huckleberry Finn, not the carefree youngster most of us have come to consider Huck but the wily and somewhat disturbing young scamp Mark Twain actually created. Would Isaac grow up to be like Huck's father, a vicious and unlovable old scavenger who never matured enough to accept any responsibility? Isaac was a charming youngster, but none of the qualities that made him such a cute eleven-year-old would seem quite so attractive if he still displayed them at twenty.

Not everyone found Isaac so attractive, even as a young boy, and he was well aware of other people's reactions, as the following poem, which he wrote when he was fourteen, indicates:

They call me Deep Dust
and they say I stink like Must
but deep down inside
I know I smell clean
like mean green.

I am not known
like I want to be
because when people walk down the street
people say
You smell
Go back to hell
Farewell.

Isaac was often a clown, but that doesn't mean he was a fool. Beneath his cavalier exterior, he sometimes suffered from acute depression. Unlike Michael, who blamed his misfortunes on society, Isaac tended to personalize his problems and accept at least partial responsibility for his own failures. He knew his lifestyle was not conducive to longevity, and he would occasionally engage in morbid ruminations about death in general and his own in particular. One day, not long after he wrote the Deep

Dust poem, I found the following unpunctuated lament scribbled on a tightly folded piece of scrap paper.

If I Die

hay people its me Isaac the coke fien the smoke fien
the pill freek now Im sick and I just might die
is it from playing hukey no its from an epidemic
and I cought it but if I die there is one thing
I would like to know will there ever be another
Isaac

Such morbidity may seem to conflict with Isaac's devil-may-care personality, but these extreme moods both reflect the passive mechanism he adopted for self-protection. Once Isaac decided he couldn't change the conditions that defined his life, he decided to roll with the punches. His toughness came out not in violent reaction but in a kind of subversive compliance. I could almost hear him pleading, "Br'er Principal, you can gib me des as much extra homework as you pleez, you can fail me an' keep me atter school, but pleez, Br'er Principal, don' suspen' me an' throw me out in de hard, col' street."

Isaac played the pliant reed to Michael's rigid oak. Each favored survival strategies which, though diametrically opposed in style, addressed similar problems. I sensed even then the deficiencies of their defenses, but we at the Youth Center didn't have any better ones to offer them. I knew that we would not be able to create individual solutions for every youngster to come along with problems similar to those displayed by my two young friends. If we were to make any progress, we would have to do so through collective action and the creation of alternative resources. Unless we could make the Youth Center into an effective vehicle for change, we would be wasting our efforts and the youngsters with whom we were working would have little chance of breaking out of the circumstances in which they were trapped.

Chapter Five

A Useful False Start

"Who are you and where are you going?" asked the stork.

"I am Dorothy," answered the girl. "These are my friends, the Tin Woodman and the Cowardly Lion. We are going to the Emerald City."

"This isn't the road," said the stork.

"I know it," replied Dorothy.

L. FRANK BAUM
The Wizard of Oz

ISAAC AND MICHAEL helped define my task as director of the Youth Center. One boy was earnest, bottled up, and angry; the other whimsical, effusive, and self-destructive. Both lacked essential skills and, from what I could tell, neither had very good prospects for survival. I felt that our program would have to address the basic problems confronting such youngsters if we were to do more than provide a place for them to hang out for a few hours when they felt like coming in off the street.

I was painfully aware from the outset how little I understood these youngsters and their world. Therefore, one of my priorities became to surround myself with people who displayed a range of insights and experiences that might enable us collectively to create responses to these complex problems. Fortunately, our organization was able to expand substantially at this time, creating the opportunity to hire some of the staff we needed and rent a couple of floors in a building near the day-care center where Hannele taught.

The key to my staff development aspirations was a young man named Arthur. Raised in the East Flatbush section of Brooklyn by parents of Jamaican descent, Arthur won a scholarship to the Trinity School at the age of fourteen. Trinity sits across a vacant lot from the building where Michael and Isaac lived, and Arthur could see the squatters working on their new homes on his way to and from school each day.

ARTHUR: Just being a black teenager in an all-white private school was enough to make me particularly conscious of my surroundings. I noticed the squatters right away, and the more I found out about what they were doing, the more impressed I became. The city had sealed up viable build-ings without having the funds necessary to demolish them or build on the site. The squatters weren't taking anyone else's homes, they were simply reclaiming adequate hous-ing from the scrap heap. Instead of waiting for someone else to solve their problems for them, they were working hard to create constructive solutions of their own. I espe-cially liked the way they utilized the various skills of so many different community members to fix up their build-ings.

Arthur first came to the day-care center as a volunteer during his senior year at Trinity. By the summer of 1971, though he was only seventeen, I offered him a position as co-director of the Youth Center. Arthur agreed to delay entering college for a year to help us develop and implement a stronger program for teenagers.

The years he spent at Trinity had isolated Arthur somewhat from what was going on in the public school system. He was dismayed to discover how poorly prepared and broadly igno-rant almost all the youngsters in our program were.

ARTHUR: There were so many things our kids didn't know: what resources were available to them, what to do if they got into trouble, even how to find their way around the city. In addition they lacked even the most superficial sense of history. We wanted to talk to them about Vietnam, but they couldn't discuss intelligently anything that hadn't happened right in their own neighborhood.

They were ready to do anything that required physical exertion, but they would rebel whenever we tried to get them to deal with matters that were abstract or intellectual. Many of them gave us the impression they didn't know how to learn. What was worse, they seemed afraid to try.

Being seventeen made it difficult for Arthur to supervise staff members, some of whom resented having to defer to someone his age, but his age had a different impact on many of the youngsters at the Youth Center. For some of these teenagers, what he was and what he represented were far more important than the often remarkable things he said or did.

MICHAEL: I saw Arthur really wanted to go to college. I knew a lot of people who tried to get what they wanted on the street, but he was the first black person I met who tried to make it the college way. Arthur would say to us, "I'm going to do this thing or that thing," and I would think to myself, "If he can do it, I can do it too."

Arthur recruited a Japanese-American schoolmate named Shigemi to work with us. Although Shigemi was still attending school full time, he began to work at the Youth Center during summers and helped out whenever he had free time after school. He was always bustling about, trying to get youngsters involved in different projects.

SHIGEMI: I have always been very political. I wanted to get involved in some activity in which I could make a positive contribution, but everywhere I turned people seemed to be working on very narrow nationalist agenda. Blacks and

45

Puerto Ricans were trying to get themselves organized and didn't want any outside involvement. Even in Chinatown I was considered an outsider.

The Youth Center, on the other hand, had all kinds of people working together, plus they were involved in day-to-day struggles, not just sitting around talking about things. It was easy to see that the people there were serious about what they were trying to do.

I guess we all had a lot of grandiose ideas at that time, and we put a lot of energy into trying to make the Youth Center a real force for progressive change in our community. If idealism and lofty goals were all you needed to make a program work, we would have accomplished great things, but we learned that structuring a program, shaping a staff, and implementing policies require technical skills many of us had not yet developed.

In addition to Arthur and Shigemi, we hired Michael's mother, Edna, and another woman from the Vernon Hotel who had settled in our neighborhood, several parents of youngsters in our program, and several other unemployed community residents who had the appropriate skills or were able to convince us they could learn them. Perhaps the most intriguing person we hired this way, and certainly the most popular, was a great bear of a man named Tony. A real hell-raiser himself as a youngster, Tony spent most of his school years in special programs designed for youngsters with serious disciplinary problems. After a stint in the army, he signed up for the police academy during the drive to increase Puerto Rican participation on the force. He enjoyed being a policeman but quit before the end of his probationary assignment when his commanding officer reprimanded him for an incident he still remembers well.

TONY: I caught some kids scrounging around inside a store that had been burned out a few days earlier. There was nothing left inside worth stealing, but they weren't supposed to be in there. I took them home and talked to their parents. I figured that way the kids would learn what they did was wrong, and they would also see we were working together with their parents to try and help them. When the captain started yelling at me that I should have arrested them, I knew I couldn't stay on the force. I just handed in my badge and walked away.

Those kids reminded me of myself at the same age. I was a real pain in the ass. Nobody could tell me nothing. I wanted to help them so they wouldn't have to go through all the problems I had. The same was true for the kids at the Youth Center. To other people maybe they were problem kids; to me they were just ordinary kids who had gotten in the habit of acting wild.

Where most of these kids came from, their parents were used to sticking pretty much with their own kind. They weren't used to seeing white and black and Puerto Rican working together. I think it really made them stop and think when they saw how close John and Arthur and I were. They weren't ever around adults who would listen to them either. For them, just being in the Youth Center meant experiencing things that were different from what they expected.

Arthur and I tried to spread responsibility around so that every staff member would feel he or she had a stake in the success or failure of the Youth Center. To reinforce this sense and demonstrate to the staff how committed we were to a democratic process, we worked out a salary equalization plan whereby everyone from custodian to director started with an equal base salary, and increments were determined by the number of dependents a worker had to support. Thus Arthur and I (he was single and my wife was working) earned the lowest salaries, while Edna, who worked as the cook, earned the highest.

EDNA: The salary equalization meant much more to me than money. It was a way of making each person feel more or less on the same level. If you want everyone to work just as hard and feel just as responsible, you got to give them an equal share of the money. If you go home with three hundred dollars each week and I go home with ninety dollars, I'm gonna say, "Why should I do any more than I have to? You want someone to put in extra time, do it yourself. I don't get paid for it."

The way it worked out, we became more like a family. If I eat, you eat. Not I eat steak and you eat beans.

Although we never made a fuss about the salary equalization with the youngsters, the effect seemed to trickle down to them as well. They realized something unusual was going on, and many of them became really curious about why we were insisting upon such a peculiar practice.

ISAAC: This kind of justice was something I had never really come in contact with. People chippin' in their salaries so that everybody would be equal, well, you just don't run into that kind of thing every day. I was used to the streets where everybody was trying to get the most for himself out of everything and didn't much care what anybody else got.

Along with equal salaries came increased responsibilities. Staff members were asked to share in hiring and firing, planning and budgeting, and all the chores necessary to develop and operate a good program. The extra work didn't sit nearly so well with everybody as the extra pay did, but the biggest problem arose from the inability of many staff members to adjust to the added responsibility. Even some of the most conscientious ones had trouble figuring out just what was expected of them.

TONY: My first two weeks on the job were horrible. Most of the time I just sat around, waiting for somebody to tell me what to do. Finally I went to Arthur and told him how unhappy I was. He said I should ask myself what I had to offer the kids. Then I should get off my ass and start organizing what I was going to do. Of course it wasn't that simple, but once I realized it was up to me to make my own contribution, everything started to click.

Sharing in the responsibility was the best thing that could've happened to me. It forced me to depend on myself, not on the boss. It made me go back into my mind and into books for ideas, and it let me concentrate on the things I knew best. I found out I was able to do much more than I expected, and I really felt good about the program and myself when something that I planned worked out good for the kids.

One of our biggest problems was finding a way to get into the public schools and influence what was going on there. So many students came to us after school virtually bursting with anger and frustration. How could we provide effective tutoring and counseling to youngsters who were so upset by the failure and humiliation they experienced all day long in school that they were ready to explode at the first suggestion that they sit down to more of the same? But the school board would not give official sanction to our program, and most teachers, perhaps rightly, saw us as a threat to their authority.

Without access to the public school system, our program floundered. We really weren't happy applying Band-Aids to the youngsters' problems, but we couldn't develop a mechanism that would allow us to intervene in a more direct and effective way. We were forced to divert our energies into developing ancillary services rather than having a direct impact on the quality of education our youngsters were receiving.

We had our internal problems as well. We had grown too fast to ensure that new staff members really understood and were prepared to implement the kinds of goals and objectives we had set for the Youth Center. Not all the staff respected the principles of shared authority and shared responsibility that went along with salary equalization. They were delighted to share in hiring new staff but wanted no part of holding their co-workers accountable for the work they were supposed to do. Many of them had too little training and too little work experience to function effectively in such a loosely structured program, and they both feared and resented the added burden of responsibility we had thrust upon them in the name of democracy.

In just over two years from the time I accepted the job as

Youth Center director, I was completely burned out. I was physically exhausted from the long hours, but that wasn't the major problem. I was emotionally drained by the welfare hotel struggle, but that wasn't the problem either. I certainly wasn't fed up with the youngsters. On the contrary, one of my complaints was that I didn't get enough time to spend with them. What really caused me such consternation was my role as administrator and staff supervisor. I had volunteered at the Youth Center and then agreed to work there because I enjoyed being with the youngsters. Now I found myself spending seventy or eighty hours a week shuffling papers and trying to get adults to perform to the best of their sometimes limited abilities.

I loved the Youth Center and its variegated staff. I loved the youngsters and the challenge of responding to their seemingly infinite problems. But the organization had become too large and unwieldy, and I could see no way, except by leaving, to liberate myself from the welter of administrative detail that was making my life increasingly miserable. Just before the end of 1972, with Arthur and Shigemi in college and Tony ensconced somewhat uncomfortably in the position of assistant director, I resigned and took my accumulated vacation leave with nothing more specific in mind than recuperating from two and a half years of hyperactivity and spending more time with Hannele.

The years I spent at the Youth Center taught me a lot, and although I came to see our efforts there as a kind of false start, they certainly helped point me in the right direction. The greatest benefit I ultimately derived from that experience, however, turned out to be the relationships I developed with Arthur, Shigemi, Tony, and the other fine people with whom I worked. They helped me discover the joy of shared struggle and a sense of community I had never before known.

Part Two

CREATING RESPONSES

Chapter Six

Putting My Money Where My Mouth Is

It is to the public school systems that 90 percent of the kids in this country are sent for their compulsory schooling, and that's where they are sorted out, including in their own heads, for the future. That's where some learn confidence in themselves and others learn they are dumb and thereby headed for a life somewhere down there below.

NAT HENTOFF
Does Anybody Give a Damn?

PULLING MYSELF physically away from the Youth Center turned out to be a much simpler task than detaching myself emotionally from Isaac and Michael. I couldn't help worrying about them. Isaac was still getting high every day, and Michael remained angry and depressed despite our efforts to help him. Both of them were enrolled in a junior high school just two blocks from where Hannele and I lived, but Isaac rarely bothered to show up, and Michael, who did attend regularly, spent most of his time in the hallways, boys' room, or principal's office.

Luther Seabrook, the principal at Isaac's and Michael's school, had been an ardent supporter of the Youth Center and a leader in the struggle for community control of public schools.

He had taken over Intermediate School 44 at a time of considerable turmoil and greatly improved the academic and social environment by breaking the large institution into minischools. Instead of tracking students according to skills or segregating them by racial or social characteristics, the minischool format allowed parents and youngsters to choose among styles of learning represented by such diverse programs as intensive reading clinic, bilingual education, and open classroom. Students could opt for skills concentrations as varied as art or dance and advanced math.

The minischool system worked splendidly for most youngsters, but there was no minischool appropriate for Isaac and Michael. They continued to drift, and I felt the school was partly to blame. One day late in January 1973, I went to Luther's office to bring this matter specifically to his attention and discovered he had already given it considerable thought.

"No one wants to work with those kids," he confided. "I tried to convince a few teachers to give it a try, but they all refused. I'm afraid if I forced one of them to take the assignment, he'd resent it and, consciously or unconsciously, take it out on the youngsters."

I asked him if he had offered anyone the opportunity to trade in all the paperwork and meetings and other administrative headaches most teachers detest for a chance to work closely with a few difficult youngsters. I suggested there must be some teachers who would prefer establishing a close relationship with even a class of students with particularly resistant problems to facing the kind of revolving-door, overcrowded classrooms they had to deal with each day. Surely the task of finding a willing teacher wouldn't be so difficult if he or she were given the freedom to design a program, choose a setting, and create conditions that were appropriate to the challenge these youngsters presented.

Luther's eyes lit up, and a Cheshire-cat smile spread slowly across his face. "Are you willing to put your money where your mouth is?" he asked.

"You know I don't have a teacher's license," I responded, suddenly suspecting I had already put not my money but my size ten and a half foot halfway into my mouth.

Luther explained that he could hire me on an instructor's line that didn't require a license. He warned that the pay was low and there was no job security, but he added that he was willing to be open-minded about working conditions. He was willing to bend Board of Education guidelines when there was justification for doing so, but I had to demonstrate how each deviation from required practice would enhance the youngsters' education and not just make my situation more comfortable.

I told Luther I wouldn't work in the school building. Some youngsters have so many negative experiences in school that even the smell of a school building means failure to them. The simple act of entering a school can transform certain otherwise normal youngsters into little percussive caps of anxiety. Luther was willing to let me develop my program out of the school building, but with the stipulation that I find and furnish a site at no cost to the school.

I didn't want supervisors interfering with my efforts to create a different type of program. I felt I needed an opportunity to succeed or fail on the basis of my own work, not on the constraints of a system that had already proved its inability to serve these youngsters effectively. Luther countered that my students would have to demonstrate significant skills improvement on standardized tests for me to maintain such independence, but he would give me a chance to show what I could do on my own at first.

I was worried about my class becoming a dumping ground for the school. I wanted the opportunity to work out a contractual arrangement with my students so they would accept some responsibility for partnership in the learning process. Luther added the requirement that I obtain written parental consent for each youngster and make sure the parents realized I was not a licensed teacher before agreeing to let me enroll their children.

I had entered Luther's office with a complaint and left with a job. I certainly had to admit the man had a flair for dealing with criticism.

Luther was getting a good deal. All he was giving up was a vacant instructorship. In return, he was getting a chance to relieve his school of some of its most disruptive students. I knew he was also taking some enormous risks. He had the authority to bring an unlicensed person into the school to assist the professional staff. It was strictly illegal, however, to assign students to an off-site program under the sole supervision of an unlicensed instructor. I will always respect and admire Luther for his willingness to take such risks in order to help youngsters no one else seemed to care much about.

The next day Luther handed me a list of students I might talk to about transferring to my class. He suggested, with a generosity I had reason to appreciate much later, that I limit my first class to five youngsters. Scanning his list I had no trouble locating several familiar names, including those of Isaac, Michael, and other youngsters who had frequented the Youth Center.

One youngster I recognized was Angelo, a hot-tempered young man who had been involved in several fights with teachers at I.S. 44 but had always gotten along well with the Youth Center staff. Angelo told me he wanted to join the class because he felt he could concentrate better in a place where he would feel comfortable. His mother, a native of Italy who immigrated to New York when Angelo was just a baby, was delighted to find someone who took a special interest in her son. Working nights in a print shop to support herself and her two children, she had already experienced more problems trying to raise Angelo than she knew how to handle.

FRANCESCA: The Catholic school where I put my Angelo at first, they kept calling me to say he wasn't grasping the work. They thought there was something wrong with him. First they told me I needed to take my baby to a psychologist. Then they told me to put him in public school because they had a better program there for children like him with special problems.

Since I'm so interested in my children's learning, I put him in public school, but the same thing happened all over again. They sent for me and told me my Angelo was doing very badly. He couldn't read a word, they said.

To me he's always been an excellent son, but in school he kinda rebels. Sometimes he would fight. The principal wanted me to pay for special tests, but at that time I didn't have no money. Besides, I didn't think there was nothing wrong with my son's brain.

Angelo, he always needed a lot of attention, but when he came home after school, that's when I had to leave for work. As far as me helping him with schoolwork, I couldn't because I'm not educated myself. He really had to grow up too much on his own. I didn't like that, but I didn't want to give up my job and go on welfare either.

My Angelo needs a teacher that cares. If he sees you don't care, he gets very upset about the whole thing and just don't pay any attention to learning. But when he sees a teacher that is interested in him, he would work, I know it.

Our experience with Angelo corroborated his mother's observations. Like so many other youngsters with whom I have worked, he responded almost exclusively to the teacher's personality and the amount of attention the teacher could devote to him. Angelo would attempt with equal enthusiasm work that was hard or easy, exciting or boring, so long as someone was standing by him with an encouraging hand on his shoulder. When the teacher had to move on to another student, however, Angelo would lapse into daydreaming or begin wandering around the room and eventually end up in trouble.

Angelo displayed so little self-confidence and so little tolerance for criticism that he would take the slightest correction from a teacher as a personal attack. Hostility would well up in him, erupting in violent outbursts that were seemingly without provocation. As a result he developed a reputation as a mean and aggressive character. Yet he was basically a lonely youngster hungering for the attention his overworked mother couldn't give him. His personal needs conflicted strongly with the kind of passive behavior the school required, and Angelo didn't possess sufficient self-control at thirteen to repress his inner drives and control his volatile behavior.

Another student Luther wanted me to speak to was Manuel, a tiny youngster who had spent most of his grade-school years in special education classes for mentally retarded children. He had been returned to regular classes the previous September, but he lacked even the most basic academic skills and was totally lost and frustrated. I tried to evaluate Manuel's reading skills informally and found he could only identify the following words: *Manuel, go, stop, yes, no, I, you, the,* and *fuck.* Of these, he could write correctly only his name.

Manuel spent much of his time playing. He was very good-natured and probably the most generous youngster I have ever known. But when he felt threatened he could unleash a tantrum of such vehemence that invariably he got his way and whoever was bothering him left him alone. Everyone in I.S. 44 thought he was crazy, but both his tantrums and his playfulness had functioned as effective defenses for him. I suspected there might be more to Manuel than he was willing to let others see.

My third candidate for class was Julio, a bright-eyed youngster with a beatific smile that made women want to cuddle him. Julio was a leader who liked to be the center of attention. Even before the class was finally assembled, he had determined he was going to be my unofficial assistant. He had previously used his charisma and leadership qualities to become one of the biggest troublemakers in the school, but I had high hopes of putting his talents to better use.

JULIO: The summer before I started going to I.S. 44, that's when I started learning about reefer and shit like that. By the time school started, I was getting high all the time. It wasn't hardly no fun in school. My friends and me, we used to meet before school and smoke a couple of joints. Then we could enjoy ourselves, making fun of the teachers and turning everything into a joke. We didn't pay no attention to learning at all.

There used to be a lotta fights at I.S. 44. I tried to be a tough dude so other kids wouldn't mess with me. Sometimes I'd get high so I wouldn't be afraid to fight. Then I'd just go wild. After a while I got a reputation, but I found out that just meant I had to fight even more.

By the time I was in seventh grade, everything was out of control. I used to walk into class and start trouble. Why? Because I knew the teacher was going to ask me to read and I couldn't. Instead of being embarrassed in front of all my friends, I'd make the teacher throw me out of the class. I didn't mind people thinking I was bad, but I didn't want nobody thinking I was stupid.

Then, when I really wanted to learn, the teachers would throw me out anyway. As soon as I'd walk into class they'd say, "The guidance counselor wants to see you, Julio." When I'd get to the guidance office, nobody'd be there. The teacher just wanted to get rid of me. I didn't really care, though. It didn't seem like school was gonna help me much anyway.

It didn't take me long to convince Michael and Isaac to join the class too, although Isaac certainly must have had some misgivings. He knew my relationship with his mother and my familiarity with his friends, hangouts, and bad habits would make it harder for him to maintain his cherished independence. Michael was still looking for someone who could transform the world into a fair and logical place sufficiently supportive to make him forget the pain and injustice of his childhood. While my class held out no such promise, he did look forward to it as a haven from the craziness he experienced elsewhere.

I now had my five students. There had been some girls on Luther's list, but I had selected only Michael, Isaac, Angelo,

Manuel, and Julio. I felt more comfortable with these rough-and-tumble boys than I would have with pubescent girls, whose sexuality might have posed problems in a mixed group. I figured the boys and I could go hiking and camping together, play ball, and if all else failed I could always let them beat up on me for a while.

I also had a place picked out for the class. The Youth Center had moved out of All Angels' Church, leaving the basement space vacant. I still maintained a good relationship with Father Eric Whiting and the vestry, and they allowed me to move in, rent free, with my five students. Julio took charge of decorations, selecting a sort of fluorescent purple paint and organizing a work crew amid much cursing and giggling. I bought some overstuffed furniture from a local dealer which, when relieved of its roach population, gave the newly painted place the aura of a funeral parlor recently converted into a clubhouse. Certainly no one wandering in off the street would have mistaken it for a classroom.

The inevitable day arrived when there was no more painting, mopping, or arranging to do, and it was time to get down to work. I had spent several years criticizing the public schools, and now I had my chance to prove I could do a better job. I had won every concession I felt was important: I had almost complete freedom to work with a small group of youngsters who had chosen to join the class. I could expect an absolute minimum of interference from the school, and I had no troublesome adults to supervise. I could devote all my efforts to helping my students. Together we would triumph over . . .

"What do we do now?" Julio asked, interrupting my reverie.

"Huh?"

"What–do–we–do–now?" he repeated.

Everyone was looking at me, waiting for my answer. I tried to think of some joke, some clever diversion, but the intimacy of our tiny group forced us to confront situations honestly, and that is what I finally had to do.

"I don't know," I admitted.

"What do you mean, you don't know?" Angelo piped up. "You're the teacher, aren't you? You're supposed to tell us what to do."

I really didn't know what we were going to do next, but that was definitely not what they wanted to hear. They wanted me to show them I was in full command, that I knew the answers to all their questions and held the solutions to all their problems, but I didn't, and there was no way to pretend I did.

Teaching junior high school youngsters is a difficult and complex business under the best of circumstances. In three short years, students must be weaned from their protective elementary school environment, given some basic skills with which to pursue a variety of academic disciplines, and prepared to cope with the demands of high school. To complicate matters, most youngsters have to navigate this transition when their bodies are undergoing a rapid and incomprehensible series of changes that leave them in a constant state of emotional turmoil.

The kind of departmentalized instruction offered at I.S. 44 constitutes a valid transitional experience for those students sufficiently mature and well motivated to settle down and focus on a different subject every time the bell rings. I would estimate that fewer than half the youngsters currently attending I.S. 44 can benefit from this kind of system. The majority, however, including the students I had chosen for my program, suffer unnecessarily from constant disruption. They need continuity of place and personnel so they can settle down, feel secure, and put their minds to the task at hand. What they need, in effect, is an upgraded version of the elementary school classroom.

Julio, for example, needed to reaffirm his tough-guy role with every teacher and every class change. Manuel would barely settle down in a class before the bell would ring again. Angelo, who needed a reaffirmation of his self-worth from every teacher, might be lucky enough to get some positive attention from two or three but would still come up short in most of his classes.

I started teaching at the time when the trend toward compensatory education was cresting and school budgets were at their fattest. Everywhere I looked, youngsters who could neither read, write, nor compute were being plugged into millions of dollars' worth of equipment that was surely providing enormous "compensation" to the companies that had stepped into this new growth industry but hardly seemed to meet the needs of youngsters craving intelligent and caring human guidance. Like the welfare hotel families, these youngsters became conduits for fantastic sums of taxpayer dollars that found their way into corporate coffers.

Our classroom had no computers, no audiovisual aids, no special learning kits. We hardly had any books. But we had several advantages other classes lacked. We had a chance to get to know each other well and learn to treat each other decently. We had a chance to create a curriculum that linked specific problems in our lives to the development of the kinds of skills that might help us solve those problems. We could make the experience as rich and rewarding as we could manage with our limited resources. Some people argued that our experience would prove nothing, for a classroom with only five students could never be cost-effective, but I have never understood how failure with thirty students is more cost-effective than success with five. Anyway, I didn't view my tiny class as a prototype or experiment. I saw it as a place my students and I could work together in a way that would be enjoyable, challenging, and rewarding for us all. There would be plenty of time later to formulate abstractions and draw conclusions.

Even with the small number of students in my charge, I harbored no illusions that my job would be easy. An incident during the first week, however, reminded me how much I had to learn. One afternoon we were all walking down West End Avenue on our way to Riverside Park. The street had been torn up by workmen replacing pipes of varying diameter and composition. My students were fascinated by the work and stopped to watch. Seizing the opportunity to get in an impromptu lesson, I asked them what the pipes were designed to carry. Someone said water, another gas, and a third electricity. They also knew steam ran in huge conduits under city streets because they saw it shooting out through manhole covers on cold days. But when I mentioned sewers I was greeted by five blank stares of total incomprehension.

I grew up in a community where every house had its own septic tank. The nearest sewer district was miles away. But even as a child I knew city kids used sewer grates as bases for stickball games. I fully expected a long and difficult struggle to improve my students' vocabulary. Had they balked at *executive, condominium,* or even *septic tank,* I would have understood. But *sewer?* Were they language poor to this appalling extent? Or, what was worse, was their experience of the world so severely limited that their tiny vocabulary accurately reflected the bounds of their universe?

I remembered Arthur's dismay over the inability of teenagers at the Youth Center to identify prominent people and places in New York City. Those youngsters had been moderately successful students. My charges were younger, more alienated, and lived in a world circumscribed by their direct personal experience and a few television fantasies. None of them had ever read a book. Their language consisted largely of action verbs, expletives, and imprecise pronouns. In order to develop a functional vocabulary and command of the English language, they would have to learn to experience the world in a totally new and different way.

I began to realize I would have to discard many of my assumptions and begin to rely more on my senses and my intuition. Only by listening, watching, and feeling for every seemingly insignificant clue concerning how my students thought and felt and responded could I hope to create a program that would be helpful to them. It wasn't that the experience of other teachers was of no value, but I had no reliable criteria by which to judge what to accept and what to exclude. I was better off letting my students guide me.

Another vignette from my first week on the job, as casual and seemingly insignificant as the sewer discussion, also left me with a lasting impression of how much I had to learn about these youngsters I had undertaken to teach. Julio and I were sitting on a wall overlooking the Seventy-ninth Street boat basin on the Hudson River late one unseasonably pleasant afternoon. He was unburdening himself to me, talking of his doubts about himself and fears about his uncertain future. Suddenly he looked up, as if he had been trying to work up the nerve to say something he felt was particularly important, and blurted out, "You know, you can't just be nice to us all the time. Sometimes you're gonna have to be strict too."

I had made it clear several times to my students that I had no intention, in a class so small, of playing policeman. We would all have to accept certain rules and agree to share responsibility for enforcing them. I answered Julio, "You have to learn to be strict with yourself. If you already know that you need discipline, you should try to find it within yourself instead of depending on me to set limits for you. After all, I won't be following you all your life, and there won't always be someone else around to keep you out of trouble."

The logic of my position is as clear and valid to me today as it was that February afternoon, but Julio wasn't seeking logic, he was searching for limits. He did need a policeman, and sooner or later, no matter how vehemently I protested, he would force me to become one. In their difficult and sometimes perilous ascent to adulthood, all these youngsters would need a judicious amount of butt-kicking to complement the encouragement and guidance I was prepared to offer. Had they been able to function in a consistently logical fashion, they wouldn't have needed my help in the first place.

As the weeks went by, I had to find a way to translate my sense of what an educational program for these youngsters should entail into something resembling a structured program. We agreed to a few rules, pre-eminent among them that no one was

Putting My Money Where My Mouth Is

to interfere with someone who was working. We had to establish the importance of respect for our hosts from the church and the building they so graciously shared with us. No drugs or alcohol were to be brought into the building, and no one was to come in high. Everyone was to come on time and be prepared to do some studying each day.

Of course, many of these rules were more often broken than followed. Isaac came when he felt like it, Julio carried drugs with him, Manuel interrupted everyone with his horsing around, and fights broke out at some point almost every day. Yet there was plenty of constructive activity going on. Angelo and Julio found books they liked and spent hours curled up in the overstuffed armchairs reading contentedly to themselves. Michael avoided reading by an almost desperate enthusiasm for math. Every time I suggested we work on a story, he would crank out a few more sheets of arithmetic. Manuel spent a lot of time playing, but he would let me pin him down for an hour a day with some reading materials, and slowly, almost painfully, he began to make some connections between the marks on the paper and sounds or words he used when speaking. Isaac slept half the time he was in class, but the other half he managed to do more work than all the rest put together.

Not all our advances were academic. Our biggest achievements involved reducing anxiety and improving the self-image of the youngsters. The person most responsible for some of the dramatic changes that occurred was a warm, motherly volunteer who walked in off the street one day and announced she intended to stay. Miriam had been working as a volunteer at I.S. 44 through a social work agency when I had "stolen" some of her favorite youngsters. Furious at first, she subsequently made up her mind to follow them and maintain the relationships she had worked so hard to build. When she saw what an open and flexible environment we had created, she left the school altogether and devoted all her free time to our class.

Miriam not only brought a lot of love to the class, she made it possible for both of us to deal with youngsters individually on a much more regular basis. Luther once suggested to me that the greatest teaching aid ever invented was the lap. If every youngster could begin reading by sitting in someone's lap, listening, watching, and imitating for as long as necessary before striking out on his or her own, the nation's reading problem would be solved. Well, Miriam's lap worked overtime as these rough, tough apprentice hoodlums curled up with her on a comfortable if threadbare couch and struggled to read whatever book they had chosen.

Gradually the youngsters stopped thinking of our classroom as school and began treating it more like an extension of home. Miriam and I became adopted aunt and uncle with whom they could share their problems. They became increasingly reluctant to leave at the end of the school day, and before long I found myself staying later and later to work and play with them. Anyone standing in front of an urban junior high school at 3:00 P.M. risks being trampled underfoot, first by some of the teachers trying to beat the rush-hour traffic out to the suburbs, and then by the children scrambling for a breath of fresh air and a little space in which to revive their cramped bodies. I had to chase my students out when it finally came time for me to leave, or they would happily have kept me there even longer into the night.

Although I was flattered by my students' eagerness to spend extra time with me, I really didn't have much for them to do in the afternoons. I approached my friend Tony at the Youth Center about the idea of spending some time with them in a little-used workshop to which he had access. Bored and frustrated with his duties as assistant director, Tony jumped at the chance to get involved in some shop and craft work with the kinds of youngsters he enjoyed so much.

I had only recruited my class in February, but already by May, according to a standardized test, Isaac had raised his reading level by nearly three years while Michael, Angelo, and Julio had improved theirs a full year over their previous year's low score.

Manuel had actually read an entire book, much to the astonishment of the reading specialist at I.S. 44, who listened to Manuel read randomly selected passages and solemnly suggested he must have memorized the entire book.

The parents of my students all spoke of miracles and heaped praise on my head for being such a wonderful teacher. The students and I knew, however, that not much teaching had taken place. The secret lay not in the teaching but in the learning. We had created an environment where learning did not depend on the teacher. With the exception of Manuel's advances in basic literacy, the youngsters had done most of the work relatively independently. Miriam and I had worked hard to encourage and reinforce their efforts, but we had really been more effective as motivators than as instructors.

My students weren't the only ones to learn a lot that semester. I learned from them much that was unexpected and revealing. I came to appreciate their surprising generosity and loyalty, qualities for which their report cards provided no slot for evaluation. I felt their capacity for trust and affection, for humor and playfulness. They had all experienced childhoods of considerable pain and disorientation, yet they responded with an inspiring resiliency that offered some grounds for guarded optimism about their futures.

Nevertheless, I had to recognize that many of them had made precious little progress where they most needed it. Michael still refused to admit his weaknesses or face his most serious problems. Isaac continued to get high and act irresponsibly despite his improved reading score. Angelo had calmed his temper while in our program, but how would he do in a regular class setting? Manuel was still depressingly infantile although his tantrums were somewhat milder and less frequent. And Julio, so sensitive and cooperative in the class, reverted to his macho persona as soon as he hit the street. Some day he would have to choose between these two stances, but at least we had a little more time to wrestle with the problem together.

Before I could get sentimental about the school year drawing to a close, my students made it clear they had also done some thinking about the immediate future. One day while we were eating lunch, Manuel asked, "Hey, John. What we gonna do this summer?"

I naively responded that I didn't know what he was going to do but I planned to catch up on some reading and take care of some badly needed repairs in my apartment. This apparently innocuous statement set off a cataclysm at the table.

"You're not gonna leave us to go back out on the street, are you?" complained Julio. "We'll probably forget everything we've learned."

"And get in trouble too," chimed in Isaac. "You know how it is when there ain't nothin' to do."

"You could take us camping," suggested Manuel. We had taken a camping trip earlier in the spring and had had a wonderful time.

"I need a job," Michael added. "Can't you get us summer jobs like you did for the kids at the Youth Center?"

Obviously my attempts to socialize these juvenile con artists hadn't stripped them of their ability to wheel and deal. They had set me up perfectly. I told them I'd think about what they were suggesting, but I knew there really wasn't anything to think about. They had already done all the thinking for me.

Chapter Seven

Ernesto: A Dramatic Approach to Combatting Failure

"It's difficult, boss, very difficult. You need a touch of folly to do that; folly, d'you see? You have to risk everything!"

NIKOS KAZANTZAKIS
Zorba the Greek

ARTHUR: Building a geodesic dome was an outrageous idea. None of us knew anything about construction. John's students were hardly a disciplined work crew. We had no money, no tools, and very little time to plan what we would do. When John first called me at college to ask if I would work with him on the project, I thought he had gone completely crazy. I also realized it would be a terrific adventure, and I wasn't going to miss out on it for anything.

Ted was the one who came up with the idea of building a geodesic dome. I suspect he had read about other people doing it and thought it might be fun to try, like raising bean sprouts in the kitchen window or dipping one's own candles. He undoubtedly saw the potential for excitement and development of diverse and useful skills, but neither he nor any of the rest of us imagined this project would swell to the almost mythic proportions it finally assumed.

69

Ted taught at the same day-care center as my wife, Hannele. He had a law degree from Columbia University and had worked in both a major Wall Street law firm and a community legal services office for several years before deciding the law had little to do with justice, and giving it up. He had carefully carved out an inconspicuous role for himself at the day-care center, but he had strong opinions and could be counted on to follow through on any project he started.

Ted was very fond of Arthur, Tony, and Shigemi and saw the program as an opportunity to work with them. Arthur, on the other hand, was thinking of majoring in education at Hampshire College and had been working part time in an alternative school nearby. He was interested in seeing if he could apply some of the educational theories he had been discussing in class to a practical situation designed for the kinds of youngsters we had worked with at the Youth Center. We had been frustrated during previous summers by external constraints placed on program size, design, and staff selection. This time we would have an opportunity to create an entire program from scratch, tailoring it in every detail to our vision of what we wanted to accomplish and the specific needs of the participants.

My semester in the classroom had strongly reinforced my sense of how inappropriate most forms of schooling are for many youngsters. No classroom was going to be able to bring the best out of Isaac and Michael, not even mine. The setting was too confining and the experience too abstract. I could try to teach them how to tolerate a certain amount of schooling and, I hoped, to acquire a few skills they needed for survival. But they were so suffused with a sense of their own failure that only experiencing some really dramatic form of success might alter their perspective on themselves and the world. Telling my students they were important and capable of great accomplishments was not sufficient to rid them of their all-pervasive sense of failure. They would have to slay the dragon of self-doubt with their own hands before they could stand and face the challenge of the adult world. Completing the dome, I felt, could serve just such a symbolic function.

The finished product, the dome structure, would embody the self-respect our program aimed to foster. The process of constructing it, however, would be at least equally important, giving cognitive and affective substance to our efforts. Our adolescent dome-builders would have to learn to measure, calculate, read plans, follow written instructions, perform tasks in proper sequence, and keep accurate records of their progress. They would also have to learn to cooperate, tolerate some frustration, delay gratification, cope with responsibility, make individual and group decisions, and develop some self-discipline. Since there was real work to be done, not the make-work tasks most summer programs had to offer, we could place real demands on our youngsters and make them stick.

We decided to limit our program to twenty participants of junior high school age: five from my class and another fifteen with similar problems who we thought would benefit from the kinds of activities we were planning. We already had a site picked out. Tony, Arthur, and I had frequently taken groups of youngsters camping on some land in the Catskill Mountains owned by the organization that sponsored the Youth Center and the day-care center. The 120-acre property afforded plenty of privacy and some stunning locations where we could erect our dome.

Even though we knew the idea of building a dome would excite our youngsters, we couldn't count on their sustained enthusiasm through all the arduous tasks inherent in the project. None of us wanted to be put in the position of struggling to coerce youngsters to fulfill their responsibilities. We wanted them to commit themselves in such a way that the project would become as much theirs as ours.

The strategy we developed to involve the youngsters fully in the project evolved from two related premises. The first, dictated by the ignorance and inexperience of the staff, was that all of us would learn and labor together. We could not afford a division of labor that effectively made some people bosses and others drones. The second was that all of us would try to lead by example rather than by command. The extent to which we could convince the participants to model their behavior on ours rather than wait for us to give and enforce orders would determine just how successful our efforts would be.

Arthur's role as director became increasingly important as the role-model mechanism became more central to our venture. For all his maturity and wisdom, Arthur was still only five years older than the youngest participant in the program. He felt some of the responsibilities he had to undertake were beyond him, placing him in a position in which he could easily sympathize with the youngsters he would be leading. He doubted his ability to write an effective fund-raising proposal, for example, and he seemed surprised and obviously pleased when the rest of us approved the draft he passed around.

ARTHUR: Being young and black, I felt hesitant about going downtown alone to meet with important people from banks and foundations, but I knew I had to overcome that reticence if I was ever going to succeed. I knew the program was depending on me to raise the money we needed, and I couldn't let my personal hang-ups get in the way. I felt really proud when a foundation president asked me who had written our proposal and I was able to answer that I had. When we went over the top on our fund-raising goal, I felt I had accomplished something as important to my own growth, in a way, as to the program.

Arthur was already an important role model for many of the youngsters who chose to participate in the program, but they could never identify completely with him. He was young and black, all right, but he had never really been one of them. He had never been an abject failure, an outcast, and from the way he carried himself and related to others it was obvious he had never doubted himself to the extent most of our program participants did. We needed someone to symbolize for all to see and understand the connection between Arthur's many strengths and the latent potential in each of the failure-prone participants who made up our work crew.

The youngster we chose to serve as that link was Ernesto, a short, athletic sixteen-year-old from the Dominican Republic with an engaging smile and a reputation for being the toughest fighter, pound for pound, in the neighborhood. Ernesto, as the saying goes, didn't take no shit from nobody. Yet beneath his cocky exterior fluttered a fragile and insecure personality.

We had given Ernesto his first job two summers before at the Youth Center. He had impressed the entire staff with his enthusiasm and leadership qualities, but as with so many youngsters who worked with us, his strengths were often overshadowed by crippling deficiencies. He could barely read or write, yet he was too proud to seek the help he needed. Unable to face the constant humiliation of failure in school, he simply stopped going. His truancy brought him into conflict with his father, and he would often stay out on the street all night rather than go home to his father's tirades.

Ernesto needed the constant praise and adulation of others to appease the ravaging inner fears and doubts that filled the place where self-esteem should reside. He took to wearing flashy clothes and gold jewelry, indulgences he could not support solely with income from odd jobs. By the time we asked him to be our crew chief, he had effectively dropped out of school and established himself as a street-level drug dealer.

ERNESTO: My father used to get down on me because he thinks I'm a loser that never had no ability of doing anything. Maybe he was trying to outgrow me from it, to make me a man, but his way of doing it was just making things worse. He used to yell at me, "You just gonna be a bum. You ain't really no son of mine." Sometimes when he'd say that I would just stay in my room and cry, it used to make me feel so bad.

One time I ran away. I lived in the subways for three

weeks, eating sodas and potato chips. I got real skinny.
Finally I had to go home. My mother cried a lot, but nothin'
changed.

School was never much for me. Mostly I went there just
to hang out. After a while I just stopped going. Instead I'd
get high and play pinball or shoot pool.

Ernesto, like so many other youngsters his age, learned to
cheat boredom with honky-tonk thrills and artificial highs, but
in so doing he cheated himself of crucial years of developmental
experiences and character building. While he skated along
precariously on the thin ice of his cool exterior image, his self-
esteem kept sinking lower and lower. Many young people who
try to support a public image of themselves they cannot in-
wardly maintain end up dead, in jail, or frightened, destructive
people. Like gamblers who keep borrowing in the desperate
hope of winning enough to cover their steadily mounting debts,
they are driven by inner panic to push themselves to increasingly dangerous acts of self-assertion. Ernesto had seen his
closest friend, trying to grow too fast and act too tough, cut
down by a gunman who turned out to be a little bit faster and
tougher. The loss stung Ernesto and scared him badly, but not
enough to make him change his ways.

Ernesto had, in fact, resolved to change — return to school,
get a job, stop getting high — many times, but he had never
been able to discipline himself to endure the long and arduous
process such change requires. He would reform for a day or two
and wonder why the rest of the world didn't immediately recognize his transformation. The first time someone looked at him
suspiciously or doubted his resolve, he would throw up his
hands and revert to his old ways, more convinced than ever that
he was destined to fail at everything but street hustling.

In designing the dome project, we took dead aim at Ernesto's
problem. Completion of the dome would require an extended
commitment to collective activity in which all the participants
would have to delay ultimate gratification for longer than they

had ever done before. Yet there would be numerous smaller satisfactions to be gleaned from every angle cut properly or panel nailed securely in place. Best of all, recognition for one's accomplishments would come not from the judgment of others but from the concrete evidence of a finished product.

Our strategy was to filter knowledge and work assignments through Ernesto. He would then divide the youngsters into work crews and see that each assignment was completed, leaving the staff free to supervise the work or solve technical problems. At this point, however, we had no knowledge to pass on to him and not the slightest idea what technical problems we were likely to encounter. Most of us didn't even know which end of the hammer to aim at a nail.

The first people we turned to for help were a group of former street gang members from the Lower East Side who called themselves CHARAS. They had built some bright pink domes, which stood out like giant pimples on the face of a vacant lot bordering the F.D.R. Drive near the Brooklyn Bridge. Whatever they knew they cheerfully shared with our staff, Ernesto, and as many of the youngsters as we could encourage to sit through the math lessons and model-building sessions. Our CHARAS friends then directed us to Joe Clinton, a building trades and civil engineering teacher at a college in northern New Jersey. Joe taught us everything from a little spherical trigonometry to subtle tricks on how to get all the pieces to fit together despite the miscalculations we were certain to make. He took us to visit a striking thirty-two-foot-diameter dome he had built with some of his students in a nearby town and capped off the tour by offering us a complete set of blueprints.

Armed with this newly acquired technology, we launched our summer program. The first week we spent at the CHARAS workshop building a sixteen-foot-diameter dome out of electrical metal tubing. After four days of measuring, cutting, drilling, and hammering, we were ready to try to assemble it in the middle of a block party on West Seventy-ninth Street. While dozens of curious onlookers milled around, Ernesto shouted instructions to his crew as they began connecting the sections of pipe. Little by little the dome started to take shape. To our surprise it took only about two hours to assemble, and the finished product was strong enough to hold up the dozens of children who immediately began climbing all over it. At first the dome-builders seemed too astonished at their own success to display much pleasure in their accomplishment, but before long they were happily explaining to anyone who would listen why the spokes of the hexagons had to be cut a different length from the spokes of the pentagons and how we were planning to build a much bigger fir-and-plywood version in the Catskills.

Our plans called for two weeks of preparation in the city, followed by a ten-day encampment in mid-July during which we would dig out the foundation and build the subfloor. We would then spend two more weeks in New York, cutting and assembling the more than one hundred triangular panels, each more than six feet long per side, which would become the twenty-foot-high, thirty-two-foot-wide dome. We would return to the construction site in mid-August to bolt the panels together and seal and paint the finished structure. Visiting Joe's dome had convinced us we had a lot of work ahead of us. None of us realized, however, just how difficult a task we were about to undertake.

The first two weeks we spent in the city passed more or less as we had planned. We spent our time forming work crews, studying blueprints, purchasing tools, making preparations for camping at the work site, and reviewing such fundamentals as how to measure a board to the nearest quarter of an inch or use a protractor to draw a precise angle. A few of the youngsters balked at making daily entries in their journals or complained that parts of the job were too much like schoolwork, but we felt confident their spirits would rise once we started actual construction.

A far more serious problem than the occasional grumbling

among program participants was a gradual breakdown in staff communication, which was threatening our flow of information and authority. The main conflict arose between Arthur and me, but the close friendships among all five of us ensured that difficulties between any two affected the other three as well.

Arthur's last-minute arrival from college just before the program began had caused him to miss most of the sessions with CHARAS and Joe Clinton. Even though he was the director of the program, I had a better grasp of the skills and information needed to construct the dome. Arthur found himself in the awkward position of being unable to lead, either by example or by direction, because he didn't really have command of where we were going. I should have found ways to pass on to Arthur what I had learned, but, as I only recognized much later, I really wasn't willing to give up control of the situation. Although intellectually committed to the idea of Arthur running the program, I was not prepared to let him make the mistakes that were a natural part of his learning to handle authority. Instead of sitting back and letting him struggle with difficult situations, I would impatiently jump in and overrule him when problems arose.

Ernesto, who should have suffered most from this confusion at the top, was having the time of his life. He was building different kinds of dome models as fast as we could supply him with materials. He couldn't really explain to others why he was cutting or attaching parts in a certain way except to say that was what he had learned from CHARAS, but his enthusiasm was so infectious that before long he had every youngster in the program trying to emulate him. That part of our role-model mechanism, at least, seemed to be working even better than we had planned.

Every evening after they finished work at their respective child-care centers, Tony, Ted, and Hannele would join Arthur, Shigemi, and me for a few beers and a meal at our favorite Cuban-Chinese restaurant. Ted, the skeptic in the group, was becoming increasingly worried about the casual way Arthur and I were preparing for the combined camping and work trip and our lack of contingency planning to handle unforeseen problems. The rest of us teased him about being so fussy and attributed his concern for detail to his years of legal training. Since he turned out to be right, however, I think it is appropriate for him to relate what happened during the first encampment in his own words.

TED: It is clear now we made certain mistakes from the outset. For starters, the program was impossibly ambitious. Twenty grown men would have been hard pressed to build the dome in one summer, given the conditions at the work site and the tools on hand.

We had chosen a site on top of the highest hill on the property, about a quarter of a mile from the nearest road. Every bit of lumber including twenty-foot-long two-by-twelves, sheets of one-inch plywood, and twelve-foot-long railroad ties had to be carried up that steep grade on our backs, not to mention the tents, food, water, and tools. Some of the kids were pretty husky fourteen-year-olds, but these tasks were enough to wear down the strongest adults.

We thought it would take us a couple of days to dig twenty holes, four feet deep, in which we could set the railroad ties as a foundation to hold up the floor. But we didn't count on rocky soil that broke our spades and sudden downpours that filled the holes faster than we could bail them out and left us knee deep in mud and nearly mad with frustration. Digging those holes alone took a full ten days.

This was the type of program you might try after you had worked with a group of kids for a long time and knew them well. Too many of these kids had never worked with us before. They had no reason to trust us, and we had all too few insights into what made them tick. To complicate matters, we foolishly took along three kids who weren't even part of the program. Counting Hannele and a friend who came along to help with the camping chores, we had thirty-two people at the campsite.

It was damned tough keeping the camp going, never mind working on the dome. The near-constant rain and the difficult conditions didn't make the kids any more cooperative either. Each new task involved an extended round of negotiations, pleadings, and threats. I think those arguments sapped our strength and morale as much as lugging sixty or seventy gallons of water up that steep and slippery hill, gathering firewood in the rain, digging latrines the kids wouldn't use. (They constipated themselves the entire time, waiting for rides into town where they could use real toilets.) All this, and then we had to try to get some work done on the dome. It was just too much to couple such demanding living conditions with the kind of work expectations we had set for the kids and ourselves.

During the first encampment we busted our butts and accomplished practically nothing in terms of the dome itself. What we all went through was an intensely human experience, horrible in many respects, rewarding, perhaps, in others, but it had nothing at all to do with our ideas of what the program should have been like.

Saturday, the day we arrived, we had to spend two hours arguing before the kids would agree to help carry the camping gear up the steep hill to the campsite. Sunday we let them explore while the staff tried to lay out the site for the dome. Monday we took half the youngsters to the dome site and started to clear away the brush. Julio and Mark wanted to go home, and Manuel started to cry because he missed his mother. Tony took the rest of the crew into town to do some shopping, and a few of them ripped off some stuff from one of the stores. They didn't get caught, but Tony was ready to throttle the lot of them when he found out. Tuesday we started digging the foundation. Half the kids immediately disappeared into the woods. One of the kids who wasn't really part of the program anyway went after another with a knife. But the kids who did stick around to

79

work put out such a terrific effort that we softened up that evening and let them have a little of our beer. Lee, at this point a fresh recruit to our program and still three years from the problems that would lead to his court appearances, had what was apparently his first drink and took off after Mark with an axe. By a stroke of incredible luck I stepped around a tent in time to grab the handle before Lee drove the business end of the axe into Mark's skull, just a few inches away.

By this time John and Arthur were hardly speaking to each other, and Hannele was practically running the campsite by herself. None of the twenty foundation holes, which were supposed to be sunk four feet into the hill, was more than twelve inches deep. Those first seventy-two hours seemed like an eternity.

The next morning the staff, including Ernesto, met in a field and decided to send some of the kids home. We called a general meeting, told certain kids they had to pack up, and gave the others a choice of leaving with them or staying to work. Ten kids got into the van, and Tony drove them back to the city.

Before that meeting I had been completely fed up and wanted to call off the whole trip, but when I saw that thirteen of the kids really wanted to stay I thought, *Who am I to say we should all go home?* I felt the kids who chose to stay had made some kind of commitment, and that helped change my attitude. I also felt relieved that after several years of working with community groups I had finally found some people who were willing to make a tough decision and stick to it.

Though we stuck it out for the remainder of the week, torrential rains kept us from accomplishing much. By the time we returned to New York we hadn't even finished digging half the twenty foundation holes. Furthermore, everyone's morale was incredibly low. The youngsters felt we were making no progress. Arthur was having doubts about his leadership ability, I was feeling guilty about my behavior, and the rest of the staff members were wondering whether we wouldn't be better off scrapping the project altogether.

I think we might have thrown in the towel then if it had not been for Ernesto. He wanted so badly to see that dome go up, and he had convinced about a dozen of the youngsters that they were going to complete the project no matter how difficult it turned out to be. Nothing seemed to dampen his enthusiasm. Within a few days of our return we noticed that most of the youngsters were talking about the trip as if it had been one of the most exciting and enjoyable experiences in their young lives. Even those who had been sent home early were boasting of all the work they had done. Somewhat reluctantly, like a couple whose marriage is breaking up but decide to try and hold the family together "for the children's sake," we agreed to carry on.

The youngsters appeared to be oblivious to the ill feelings that plagued the adults. Looking back, it seems as if two separate programs had been taking place simultaneously: One, inhabited by nervous and unhappy staff members, resembled a nightmare; the other, animated by Ernesto and his crew, consisted of calamities, which seemed to evaporate with the rain, as well as good times, sometimes more imagined than real, that etched themselves indelibly in their memories.

Between encampments we reorganized our crews and developed a new set of tasks for the youngsters we had sent home early. Many of them now begged to be reinstated to the main crew, having completely forgotten how miserable they had been the previous week, but we held fast. We still had to complete those holes before we could set the foundation, and we knew a smaller crew would be more effective. The next weekend, cheered by a good weather report, we took an unscheduled trip to the dome site to try to finish the remaining holes.

This time staff and participants took out their frustrations on the hill instead of on each other. Ernesto sensed what the rest of the staff members were going through and took upon himself the task of seeing that the workers put out their best effort. He was everywhere, giving encouragement, prying out stubborn bits of rock, and making sure no one was tempted to let down before we were all ready to stop. Our crowbars drove like jackhammers into the clay and rock. When the holes got so deep that our spades couldn't turn to lift the loose dirt out of the bottom, Ernesto, Michael, and some of the other strong workers picked up Isaac and the other skinny ones and lowered them head-first into the holes to scoop out the final inches by hand. As the sun began to set Sunday evening, we raced to pour the last load of cement into the twentieth hole and wedge the last railroad tie into an upright position. We had wrung our first victory from the stubborn hill. Piling into the van to go home, we felt we had reached a turning point. The second full encampment, after two uneventful weeks in the city, found us better prepared and better organized. The youngsters understood their responsibilities better, and the staff had a better grasp of the work that needed to be done. We were also finished with the most unpleasant part of the job and could look forward to more carpentry and less boring labor.

The reduced work crew was still not prepared to put in a full week at maximum effort, but a few youngsters were always willing to do more than they were asked. Despite the ripening blueberries, which hung in clusters from the shoulder-high bushes surrounding the work site and provided a powerful distraction in the long August afternoons, we managed to build a remarkably level platform nearly thirty-five feet in diameter on our foundation. Eventually it would be the floor of the finished dome, but at this stage of construction it sat unadorned some six feet above the ground at the steepest part of the slope, looking like some kind of extraterrestrial launching pad for flying saucers. The view from atop it down the undulating valley toward the Delaware River was spectacular.

We were understandably pleased when a group of local builders whom we invited to inspect our work expressed astonishment that untrained teenagers could have helped build such a craftsmanlike structure, especially without the use of power tools. Digging those blasted holes had been donkey work, a sheer triumph of determination and backbreaking labor. This platform, however, with its intricate radial pattern of beams and transverse joists, was an object of great beauty and the first tangible evidence that our efforts were beginning to bear fruit. None of the youngsters or staff who worked on that platform could look at it without feeling tremendous pride in what we had accomplished.

Being part of the work crew became a mark of distinction in our community. People I hardly knew would approach me to ask if we were really building a dome in the country and marvel at the change in attitude among the youngsters who were working with us. We became known as the people who were building the dome, and gradually our youngsters began referring both to themselves and the program as The DOME Project. Curiously, those who were not permitted to return to the work site seemed to take almost as much pride in their association with the project as those who had actually finished the platform. To all of them the experience was special, an opportunity to play a role in accomplishing something no one believed we could do.

By September our problem was no longer whether we would complete the dome but when. Less than four months had passed since my students had confronted me with their need for a summer program, and the actual construction project had spanned just eight weeks. We had accomplished slightly less than half of what we had set out to do, but we could attribute that shortfall at least as much to overly optimistic planning as to poor implementation. Even crack construction crews have to take into account potential problems that can be caused by inclement weather or difficult terrain, but we had innocently assumed we could simply make a timetable and stick to it.

With the end of summer vacation, Tony and Ted had to

return to work, Shigemi went back to college, and our workers trudged reluctantly off to school. Arthur and I had settled our differences to the point where he decided to take a semester's leave from college to develop a math program for my class. He had been deeply troubled by our youngsters' inability to handle simple computation. At college he had been impressed with the importance attached to statistics and the use of computers, even in the social sciences. He knew that many black and Hispanic youngsters were being steered away from math and science courses at an early age, and he worried about the consequences this tracking might have on their future choice of careers.

ARTHUR: Up to that summer, I never thought of myself as much of a mathematician. But watching our kids struggling to make even the simplest measurements, I began to realize how important it is for black and Hispanic children to master concrete skills in science and math. I sensed a reluctance on the part of teachers at all levels, from elementary school through college, to encourage us to enter those areas of study. We were being cut off from the mainstream of technology, and, what was worse, we were cooperating in our own isolation. I myself had felt reluctant to push for admission to difficult math and science courses in high school and allowed myself to be scheduled for classes that left me at a disadvantage in college and with a strong sense of inferiority when comparing myself to people with any kind of technical expertise. I understood what our dome builders were going through, and I started to feel a responsibility to make some efforts to begin breaking down the barriers that were keeping us on the outside looking in.

Arthur wanted to spend a semester in the classroom to get a better idea of the kinds of problems he would have to face. The experience must have served its purpose, for when Arthur returned to Hampshire he dropped his education major and eventually went on to earn a master's degree in math from the University of Michigan.

Arthur wasn't the only dome-builder whose life changed as a result of that summer's experience. Ernesto, who had been drifting toward serious trouble before we offered him the crew-chief position, showed little inclination to return to the street. With a minimum of effort, Arthur and I were able to convince him to enroll in West Side High School, an alternative public high school just a few blocks from our program's headquarters. West Side offered the kind of supportive environment we hoped would nurture Ernesto's resolve to return to school. The school was also small, so he could get the attention he needed without having to show off or adopt behavior that conflicted with his inner feelings.

Most days after school Ernesto and a few of the other dome-builders would join Arthur and me at our makeshift workshop in a nearby building. There we learned to cut compound angles to within a thirty-second of an inch, concoct makeshift jigs for our drill press, and cut plywood sheets to the exact dimensions specified by our blueprints. Ted would usually join us when he got through work, and the staff members would often work long hours into the evening after the youngsters had gone home. The work was tricky and dangerous, the working conditions wretched, and all of us seemed always to be exhausted. We had gone straight from the summer program to the classroom without a break, and the pressure began to take its toll by midwinter.

Arthur and I had doubled the size of our junior high school alternative class from five to ten. In addition, we were still working closely with Isaac, Ernesto, and other members of the program who were in high school. Lee, who had come so close to killing another youngster with an axe during the summer, had entered high school in September, but by November he had walked out, swearing never to return. Instead of hitting the streets the way most youngsters would upon walking away from school, he came directly to our class, picked up a book, and began to work. When I asked him what was up, he announced he had joined our class. If we let him stay, fine. If not, he wasn't going to attend school at all. I tried to get him to elaborate, but all he would tell me was that something had happened that he didn't want to talk about.

He seemed eager to cooperate, and we knew him to be a willing worker. In fact, despite the axe incident, we all liked and respected Lee. After talking to Lee's mother, Arthur and I decided to let him stay in the class for as long as it would take to convince him to try West Side High. He ended up staying with us the rest of the school year, getting no credit for his attendance (ours was a junior high school class, and Lee had already started high school) although he never missed a day and did his work much more conscientiously than most of the students officially assigned to us.

Crises such as Lee's were all too common. It seemed someone was always in some kind of predicament that required our immediate attention. Miriam still came around regularly, but even so we were often overwhelmed. Perhaps we would have had an easier year if some of our students had reverted to their prior habits of truancy, but they came every day, often bringing a friend with a problem they had promised we would solve.

In January Arthur returned to college. The prospect of his departure had me understandably upset until Shigemi told me he was considering taking some time off from college and suggested he would be willing to take Arthur's place. He already knew all the youngsters, had all the requisite skills, and made it possible for us to move into the second half of the school year with a minimum of disruption. We still spent our evenings cutting, drilling, gluing, and nailing dome panels, although our original lofty goals and developmental strategies were rapidly being replaced by an intense desire to finish the project any way we could.

*

We had begun building the dome with the intention of proving to our youngsters that they could successfully undertake a challenging project. Had we abandoned the project when the first encampment turned sour, we could have written off the whole venture as a bad idea, but by the spring of 1974 we had put too much into it to allow it to fail. If we ever doubted how important it was for us to finish, Ernesto was always there to remind us. I am convinced to this day that he would have done absolutely anything within his power to see that dome completed. We simply could not let him down.

On April 30 Hannele found a way to divert my attention from dome panels and the problems of my students: She gave birth to our first child, Mikko Jonathan. I was with her during the delivery and walked around for days with a foolish grin on my face, trying hard to remember I was not the only person in the world to experience the wonder of becoming a father. As a gift for Hannele, I promised to take the summer off so we could go to Finland and introduce Mikko to the European half of his family.

Arthur and Shigemi agreed to run the summer program in my absence, but before I left I wanted to see the dome completed. We figured it would take three days of hard work to assemble the basic structure. The rest of the summer could be spent sealing and painting it plus adding doors, steps, and numerous other details. All our plans would have to be scrapped, however, if we couldn't make the panels fit together, and I was still the one who knew the most about how to get that done.

The day after school ended, Ernesto, Michael, and I loaded the more than one hundred panels into a rented truck and took off for the Catskills. We unloaded the truck at the bottom of the hill and then took a quick run up to the dome site to confirm that our platform had survived the severe winter intact. Not a single railroad tie had heaved up on us. Crossing our fingers that scavengers and vandals wouldn't discover our supplies before we returned, we drove excitedly back to the city.

The following Thursday evening, Arthur, Ted, Tony, Shigemi, Ernesto, and I piled into two vans with our thirteen remaining crew members and headed upstate to erect the dome. We pitched camp expectantly that warm June evening, our minds awash with vivid memories of past encampments and images of how the completed dome would look. There was much less horseplay than usual at the campsite, and by nightfall all the tents were quiet as we tried to get a good night's sleep.

The next morning we enthusiastically set to work at the dome site, bringing up all the panels and erecting the scaffolding. Right after lunch we bolted on the first row of panels. It took a while for the youngsters to learn how to match adjoining sides of the giant triangles, and we spent much of the afternoon undoing mistakes and making sure we had every component properly placed and secured. Nevertheless, by the time darkness forced us to halt, we had assembled enough of one side to create a shape like a giant sail against the summer sky.

That night I didn't sleep at all, as powerful winds whipped and howled across the hilltop, creating visions in my head of that sail taking off and soaring into the next county. I doubted our flimsy braces could withstand the force of the storm and cursed myself for not having prepared properly for this kind of situation. There was nothing I could do, however, but toss and turn in my sleeping bag and wait for the night to end.

Morning found all the panels miraculously still in place. The wind had subsided, and the hill was shrouded in a cold, gray mist. A light mountain rain tapped against our ponchos as, with a deep sigh of relief, we set to work. The drizzle made the scaffolding slippery, but our young workers carefully hoisted the cumbersome panels into place and bolted them fast. We were all enchanted with this giant Tinker Toy, and our spirits rose with each completed ring of panels. I knew, however, that our panels were not all uniform. Joe Clinton had warned us that errors of as little as half an inch could make it impossible for us to fit the last panels in place. The more excited the youngsters became, the more I worried about the panels we had cut in haste and what we would do if the last ones wouldn't fit.

The rain came at us steadily the entire day, numbing our

hands and limiting the amount of work we could accomplish. By the time darkness forced us to call it a day, we had fastened fewer than half the panels. We were chilled to the bone. We needed hot showers and good hot meals, but we had to settle for washing in the lake and eating the sandwiches prepared in advance to keep camp chores to a minimum. Dead tired, we crawled into damp sleeping bags and tried to get some badly needed rest.

Sunday morning broke sunny and still. Ernesto led the charge to the campsite and assigned tasks to the eager workers. The dome was beginning to take shape; already its spectacular geometry could be seen rising above the trees from the valley below. The nearer to the top we worked, however, the more our problems multiplied. The scaffold got higher and more precarious. The panels had to be raised farther off the ground and held at sharper angles to the scaffold while being bolted in place. As I feared, it became harder to fit each succeeding panel into its allotted space as the tolerance for error grew smaller. The youngsters had to tug and push with all their might to align the awkward panels.

The orange light of late afternoon turned the dome's plywood surface to burnished gold. I nervously paced the platform, worrying about the remaining few panels. Problems kept arising, but somehow we overcame each one. By this time we were all oblivious to hunger, fatigue, and, to a certain extent, each other. There was very little conversation. Everyone's attention was riveted on the narrowing gap that separated the uppermost panels.

By nightfall we made it to the apex pentagon, the final five panels that would close the sphere. Drawing on reserves of energy we didn't know we possessed, we increased the feverish tempo of our work. The first two panels slipped into place with surprising ease. But the third panel put up a stiff fight, and my poor, nervous stomach began feeling the way it had when Hannele went into labor.

I could no longer stand watching from below and climbed the

scaffold to have a hand in securing the final panels. It was too dark to work safely now, but no one thought of stopping until those last two panels were bolted down. We attached lanterns to the top of the scaffold and kept going. All the workers who weren't actually on the scaffold were standing around the platform, their eyes glued to the space twenty feet above them where the final drama was unfolding. With a tremendous amount of pounding, pulling, and straining we were able to attach the fourth panel. Only one remained.

Arthur, Michael, and Ernesto were lying on their backs on the top of the scaffold, pushing up and out with their legs on crucial points, trying to make more room for the final panel. It rested uneasily over the space where it was to be fastened, one edge in place, the other two overlapping the seams into which they would have to fit. I was standing in the center of the scaffold, my head and torso thrust up through the ventilating hole in the last panel, flailing away at the edges with a sledgehammer, trying to force the panel down far enough for Arthur and Ernesto to slip in the final bolts.

It may have taken only five minutes, but it seemed like hours. I remember feeling that my arms would fall off before that panel would ever budge. Half in the dome and half out, watched by the incandescent stars above and the eyes of the weary but excited youngsters below, the cool night air prickling my sweat-drenched body, I experienced a kind of mystical transformation. The wooden pentagon I was struggling to complete was no longer an inanimate structure but the friendship of five staff members — a friendship that had taken a terrible pounding, had threatened to come unstuck, but that this effort, if successful, would render whole again.

I heard a shout from below and looked down to see Arthur drive home the final bolts. The wound was closed. It was nearly midnight, but we could have turned off all the lanterns. The glowing faces of our exhausted but happy band of dome-builders were quite sufficient to light up the countryside.

Arthur had been right: Attempting to build a geodesic dome

with a crew of undisciplined and failure-prone adolescents was outrageous. A less committed staff would have dropped the project in its infancy; a wiser one never would have started. Yet we had faced many kinds of adversity and emerged as winners.

The completion of the dome was a watershed experience for Ernesto and many of the other participants. It created a strong bond among them and with the staff. It showed them how much we could all accomplish by working together, but in even more important ways it gave each of them a sense of personal achievement and worth. Ernesto told me, "The main point is that we proved a bunch of guys like us who never been serious about nothin' in our lives can really do somethin' if we try. Building the dome was fun, but finishin' it, that was like gettin' a diploma."

The dome became a useful symbol for our program: an alternative shelter where every structural member contributes equally to the strength of the whole. We never built another dome, but the name *The DOME Project* stuck with us. Some people find it a curious name for a youth program, but it serves as a reminder of the kind of unconventional activity that established us as a group willing to take great risks to prove to our youngsters that they can succeed in life despite histories of chronic personal failure.

Chapter Eight

Ramon: A Persistent Approach to Combatting Failure

In order for the oppressed people to be able to wage the struggle for their liberation, they must perceive the reality of their oppression not as a closed world from which there is no exit, but as a limiting situation which they can transform.

PAOLO FREIRE
Pedagogy of the Oppressed

SOME YOUNGSTERS DEVELOP such a deep-rooted sense of themselves as failures that they become virtually crippled. Too frightened and passive to participate in any project designed, as the effort to build the dome had been, to demonstrate in a dramatic way their potential for success, they need to be nursed along in a gradual and almost therapeutic manner. Such a youngster was Ramon, singled out and referred to us by an assistant principal in I.S. 44 who realized that Ramon needed special attention his teachers couldn't provide.

RAMON: I had no confidence when I was little. I wouldn't even go to the store by myself. I was afraid the owner might give me the wrong change on purpose and then laugh at me 'cause I wouldn't be able to tell. I was afraid I would never be worth nothing, not even for picking up garbage or something like that. And by not having respect for myself, it was like throwing my life away. Already by seventh grade I had started giving up.

Ramon tried to compensate for his sense of insecurity by dressing and talking like a tough guy. He wore a cut-off Lee jacket with crossed swords painted on the back, a red bandana knotted around his forehead, studded engineer boots, and he carried a heavy chain through a belt loop in his jeans. He was so tiny, however, that his outfit made him infinitely more comic than threatening.

Ramon had been raised in Puerto Rico, the sixth of eight children. His parents' marriage had broken up soon after the birth of the last child, leaving his mother to raise all the children alone. Uneducated and unskilled, she had a hard time providing even the barest essentials for her family.

RAMON: When we lived in Puerto Rico, we couldn't even afford shoes, and we had to walk miles just to get to school. My mom used to work carrying loads of firewood on her back for long distances, with no shoes, over the sharp rocks in the road. Still she couldn't earn enough. Sometimes we couldn't go to school 'cause we didn't have no clothes to wear.

Unable to make ends meet or educate her children properly, Ramon's mother convinced an uncle who was living in New York to send for her and the children. She found an apartment in a run-down tenement on West Eighty-eighth Street and a job in a sweatshop in the Bronx, but her dream of a decent education for all her children foundered on the harsh realities they encountered in New York. One by one, the older children dropped out of school until only Ramon and the two youngest remained.

Ramon had a tremendous desire to succeed in school, but the schools he attended very nearly extinguished it. He had not been brutalized by his environment, nor had he fallen prey to the destructive allure of street life. True, he had known nothing but poverty all his life, but he had a loving family and a strong sense of personal values. His history suggests that the problems he was experiencing in school by the time he came to us in seventh grade grew, at least in part, out of the inability of earlier schools and prior teachers to deal with his needs adequately from the time he arrived in New York.

RAMON: The first school I went to was P.S. Twenty. It was hard for me because I didn't speak English, and they didn't have bilingual classes. I was in third grade. I just sat there all day like a dummy 'cause I didn't know what was going on. Then I began to make a few friends, and they started teaching me some words in English, but even that caused me some problems later because most of them didn't speak good enough to teach me the right way.

One time, when I was in fourth grade, I didn't have a pencil. The teacher started yelling at me that if I didn't have a pencil, she didn't want me in her class. I tried to tell her I wanted to stay, I just didn't have a pencil. Maybe she never knew what it was like to be poor, I don't know. Instead of letting somebody share with me, she called the monitors and sent me to the principal. On the way, the monitors pushed me down the stairs. I hit my head, and then I got dizzy and started to cry. The principal just gave me a note and sent me home.

After that I kept getting terrible headaches. Every time I tried to read, my eyes would start watering and my head would ache like someone was hitting it. I couldn't concentrate at all. Going to school became something like going to the toilet. You do it because you have to, but you don't get any enjoyment from it.

I questioned Ramon closely about his headaches. He said his mother had taken him from clinic to clinic, but the doctors had found nothing wrong. He insisted he had suffered what he called brain damage in his fall, yet I was highly suspicious of a condition that doctors couldn't diagnose but whose symptoms were activated every time Ramon picked up a pencil or a book. I thought he might have latched onto this supposed injury as an involuntary defense against recurring failure, and I strongly suspected a little success would be worth more than a renewed cycle of clinic visits.

Ramon was so highly motivated that it was a pleasure to have him in class. I found it terribly frustrating to deal with his headaches, whether real or imagined, but I soon began to realize they provided the key to helping Ramon become a successful student and self-confident adult. He had internalized and even physically integrated a sense of himself as a failure to the point where he was willing to view himself as physiologically impaired. In an equally deep part of his psyche, however, he had refused to accept this view of himself as such a severely limited person, and the tension caused by these conflicting views was very possibly causing the headaches. We had to tap that part of Ramon that had not given up on himself if we were to help him pull out of the depressed state he experienced whenever he began thinking about his future.

RAMON: When I first started trying to read, I used to buy comic books. It would take me a week to finish even one page, and then I wouldn't really understand it. Once I even burned a comic book, I got so mad, but later I thought about it and realized it wasn't the comic book's fault, it was mine.

I didn't want to be hanging out all my life. I wanted to have a good job and raise a family. I wanted to know how to do lots of things, to read newspapers, to know what was happening. The way things were, I couldn't even read *TV Guide* to know what good programs were on. I didn't want to spend my whole life flipping from channel to channel.

Every day I would make sure I put aside at least an hour, even if it had to be lunch hour, to read with Ramon. He was always willing to cooperate, but, oh, those headaches! They would start

95

the first time he ran up against a word he couldn't recognize easily. His eyes would start to water, and he would complain the pain was too great for him to continue. At first I would let him take a short break and try again later, but the same word was always waiting for him when he returned, so there was usually no improvement. I tried convincing him that his reading problems caused the headaches, but he insisted it was the other way around. I became increasingly impatient with the headaches and urged Ramon to work through them, but I always pushed gently with one arm around his shoulder. There was no question in my mind that the pain he felt was real, even though we disagreed on the cause, and I was equally convinced that it would disappear once Ramon realized he was perfectly normal and could learn as well as anyone else.

Ramon really presented me with a kind of chicken-and-egg dilemma. I couldn't convince him he could learn to read until I showed him some results, and I couldn't show him any results until he began to believe he could learn to read. I don't know which of us was the more eager for him to succeed, but both of us were persistent enough in our efforts to create some encouraging movement.

RAMON: My first days in The DOME Project class, I didn't really think it would be any different from I.S. Forty-four. But when I began to notice how the other guys were taking their work seriously, it sort of opened something up in me. I thought this might finally be a real school where I could learn. In the beginning I couldn't read even one word, but I started learning sounds, and then a couple of words, and then I read this little story about a farmer and a volcano. It wasn't until I finished the whole story that I started to think, *Hey, maybe I can learn to read after all.*

It may sound funny, but when John got mad at me, it made me feel good. I knew it was because he was trying to help me. Teachers in other schools never did that. They just said, "O.K.," and let me go. That told me they didn't care so much, and I just stopped trying. John wouldn't accept my excuses, and somehow that made me try harder. I knew he wouldn't keep after me like that if he didn't think I could make it.

I don't think it is an oversimplification to suggest that all the other schools Ramon attended in this country made him feel inferior and alienated from the society into which his mother had introduced him. Not surprisingly, his mother felt equally isolated, both by her inability to speak English and her sense that she could never really be accepted by American society. While she never made excuses for herself or her children, I knew she felt they were all struggling against unfair odds, which she had done nothing to create.

Most of the parents with whom I have worked share similar views. They don't trust their children's teachers and don't feel comfortable in their children's schools. Teachers often complain that parents don't come for school conferences, and many large schools can't draw a handful of parents to regular Parents' Association meetings. Yet most of the parents of DOME Project students support our program enthusiastically and turn out in impressive numbers for meetings, fund-raising benefits, and other activities for which we request their participation. They find many ways to let us know how sincerely they appreciate our efforts to help their children, and they are almost always willing to back us up in whatever ways they can. Why, then, do the same parents feel so alienated from the public school system that is supposed to serve their children?

I know my own parents never felt unwelcome in the schools I attended or estranged from the school system. My schoolmates and I may not have liked some of our teachers, but we never saw them as different from the other adults we knew. Our parents and teachers belonged to the same religious and civic organizations, shopped in the same stores, and visited each others' homes. If one of us was bold enough to admit at the dinner table that he had been punished in school, he could usually expect more of the same from his parents. As adolescents we all had good reason to respect the solidarity of the adult alliance arrayed against us.

There were no nonwhite teachers in our suburban Westchester school system, but that was hardly surprising, for there was only one black child in any of the Pleasantville schools. Our town was tiresomely homogeneous, although there were some Italians who lived in "The Flats" by the railroad tracks and Jews who were moving into the unincorporated tract just beyond village limits. As youngsters we were vaguely aware of social and ethnic differences, but they certainly mattered less to us than the ability to hit a curve ball or do the latest dance.

New York City, on the other hand, has a remarkably diverse population. Of the nearly one million youngsters registered in its public schools during the 1978–79 school year, approximately 39 percent were black, 30 percent Hispanic, 29 percent white, and the remainder Asian and other. In contrast, 84 percent of the public school teachers were white while only 11 percent were black and 5 percent Hispanic. Segregated housing patterns dictate that while whites dominate the teacher corps in every district, some schools have a majority of white students while many others have none or only a few. All elementary and junior high school students must live in the district surrounding their schools; a substantial number of teachers don't even live in the city. I am not one of those who believes white suburban teachers cannot or should not teach nonwhite inner-city youngsters. However, the imbalance that exists in many schools, where a predominantly white staff works with a predominantly or exclusively nonwhite student body, is unhealthy and racist, by implication if not by design.

Teachers function as role models for their students. White teachers can work effectively with nonwhite students, but a strong argument can be made that they should not be the only or even the principal role models available to such youngsters. A nonwhite child looking around his or her school and seeing only white faces in positions of authority has to suffer some sense of incongruity, even though the full impact may not be felt until years later.

Nevertheless, a school can still accomplish worthwhile objectives, even with a racially inappropriate staff/student distribution, so long as teachers and students can achieve the level of mutual respect essential for the minimal functioning of a classroom situation. Unfortunately, many teachers, demoralized by increasing class size, the erosion of job security, and a perceptible decline in the respect their position commands, are merely putting in time until they can draw their pensions. They no longer have the desire or energy reserves needed to meet their students halfway. Yet it is virtually impossible to remove teachers from the classroom against their wishes, presuming they have sufficient seniority to withstand the lay-offs induced by budget cuts. Laws and contract stipulations designed to prevent arbitrary or politically motivated firings now effectively protect teachers from removal for incompetence, dereliction of duty, or even demonstrable misconduct.

Over a decade ago, New York City erupted into turmoil as parents in many poor communities demanded community control of their schools, and the teachers' union countered with a citywide strike that shut down all the schools. The community control forces argued that the population of the city was too diverse for centralized policies to be effective. They wanted more say in hiring and firing staff, selecting curricula, and determining local school policy. Although community control proponents won some concessions and an elaborate mechanism consisting of thirty-two local school boards, the new system was eviscerated before it ever began to function. The central Board of Education retained negotiating power with the teachers' union, ultimate fiscal control, and the power to license school personnel. The local boards were left to quibble over the distribution of discretionary funds and absorb community anger or deflect it away from the central board.

Community control is no longer the stirring battle standard

around which people rallied in the sixties in an attempt to make the institutions in their lives more responsive to their particular needs. One reason, I suspect, is that many people ultimately had too much difficulty defining their community. New Yorkers who saw community as a racial or ethnic group too often found themselves engaged in bitter factional struggles for power within that group. Others began to realize that while they might shop in their immediate neighborhood they generally worked in another. Neighbors might socialize with one group, attend church with a second, and send their children to school with the offspring of a third. Such people belong to many communities, and the interests of one group might well conflict with those of another in the narrow and parochial struggles being waged for institutional power.

Our society lacks class harmony and a common culture. Consequently our institutions work well for some who rely on them and poorly or not at all for others. Many of our young people, particularly among the poor and nonwhite (although by no means exclusively so), have become unstable repositories of this cultural confusion. Daring and frightened at the same time, passive in some ways and aggressive in others, they disrupt our schools and terrorize our neighborhoods. Through it all, we go on blaming these youngsters as if they had somehow chosen this role, from among several, as the most desirable for themselves.

In fact, the choice has usually been made for them. Did Michael choose to spend his childhood in the Vernon Hotel and similar slums? Did Isaac select his mother for her permissiveness or Ernesto prefer a father who made him feel worthless? We may find it convenient to blame our social victims for their problems, thereby absolving ourselves of any responsibility for their condition. Public institutions, however, and public schools in particular, must undertake to serve all who seek help, regardless of the prior conditioning they bring to the experience or the limitations society has imposed upon them.

Michael Rutter and his research team, in the recent book

15,000 Hours, argue persuasively that schools can have a significant impact on a youngster's academic achievement and school
behavior. The Rutter group's research indicates that there are
good schools and bad schools and that attending one or the
other can influence substantially the results a student is likely
to achieve. Of the twelve inner-city London schools studied by
the team, after adjusting all data to ensure that the student
populations were similar in almost every controllable respect,
the worst students in the most effective school scored as well or
better on achievement tests and displayed as good school behavior as the best students in the worst school.

Sometimes a visitor can learn a lot about a school just by
walking into the building. Schools in which classrooms are
open, children have considerable freedom to make choices, and
teachers serve more as facilitators than monarchs, convey a
certain respect for the child's role in the educational process.
Schools that emphasize a more passive role for their youngsters,
having them sit obediently and quietly in class while the teacher
directs each lesson, correspond to a view of the child as unformed matter or empty vessel needing to be shaped or filled
by the wise pedagogue. I have also visited schools with much
different concepts of their mandate. In one Manhattan school
for "difficult" children, I found students lined up by height in
little platoons, carefully watched by an adult brandishing a
pointed stick with which he alternately rapped his charges on
the back of the leg to keep them in line and signaled those who
were to enter the cafeteria for lunch. Since the army has become
increasingly reluctant to accept youngsters with such poor academic and behavioral records, I can only assume these youngsters were being trained not for the rigors of military life but for
prison.

Yet, in many ways, the saddest situation of all occurs in those
schools in which the students are apparently being prepared for
nothing at all. They are simply being warehoused. The restless
ones roam the halls, gamble in the bathrooms, fight in class, or

smoke dope in the schoolyard. Meanwhile, their more passive classmates are being plugged into expensive machines, spending long hours of each school day being programmed to distinguish "correct" answers from among several choices.

What does our society expect from these young people? Having allowed them to reach adolescence with no appreciable skills, it clearly doesn't expect them to fulfill an intellectual function. Having identified them as culturally deprived, it isn't grooming them for cultural leadership. Having defined them as socially inferior, it cannot consider them socially valuable. It needs them less and less for manual labor. Shifts in technology and widespread unemployment have even stripped them of their potential value as cannon fodder or members of a wage-dampening reserve labor pool.

The sad answer is that we don't expect anything from these youngsters. They happen to be here, these descendants of slaves and colonized peoples, so they must be fitted into the system somewhere. In the days of worldwide American hegemony, limitless frontiers, and expanding American markets, there always seemed to be a job and a place in society for anyone willing to step forward and claim it. Those days, it appears, may have gone the way of the twenty-nine-cent gallon of gas. Yet the youngsters remain, and what our school system is doing to them constitutes a tragedy of enormous proportions.

Often the youngsters realize what is happening to them but are powerless to correct the situation. Ramon, for example, understood all too well what society expected from him. Until he came to The DOME Project, he dressed and acted the part to the hilt. But the resiliency I admire so much in the youngsters I work with prevented Ramon from believing totally in the image society had encouraged him to create for himself. Although he thought of himself as a failure, some part of him still wanted to believe he could succeed.

Ramon would never have gone with us to build the dome. He wouldn't even go with us on one-day field trips at first. Anything new or different from the routine of his daily existence posed a threat that he would doggedly avoid. Clearly we could not count on creating some dramatic event or single mind-expanding experience to transform Ramon into a self-confident person. We would have to work very patiently and persistently with him, gradually breaking down his reluctance and self-doubt while slowly building up his skills and self-confidence.

*

Ramon needed much more help than we could provide in the classroom so I began urging Bob to spend some time with him. Bob, whose own children were in college, had grown up in a tough section of the Upper West Side and still lived just a few blocks from the church basement where we were teaching. He had dropped out of school at sixteen to ship out with the merchant marine and later studied electronics at the old RCA Institute. Now he was an independent sound system installer and repairman who seemed to spend more time working with local street kids than repairing stereos. He later told me that discovering our program made him feel as if he had found a spiritual home for himself and the youngsters he had taken under his wing.

Bob and I raised enough money to buy a few electronics kits, and twice a week he turned our classroom into a workshop. In addition, a couple of afternoons a week Bob would take Ramon on house calls.

RAMON: I had always liked working with my hands. I used to try to fix things around my house, but most of the time I'd just take them apart and then couldn't get them back together again. When I started working with Bob, I got so excited I just didn't want to stop. I felt I had found something like a treasure.

Sometimes I would have to go with Bob to a customer's apartment. We'd come to some fancy building and the doorman would say to Bob, "Mrs. Jones left you the keys

to her apartment and said to go ahead and fix her stereo."
I would think, *Wow! To be trusted like that you really have to show
people you are worth something.* Later, we'd be working on the
stereo in this apartment with all this rich stuff in it and Bob
would just leave me alone to go to some other part of the
apartment to fix some wires or something. He seemed to
be telling me I could be trusted just like him. That was
better than having a hundred dollars in my pocket.

Bob couldn't be absolutely certain, of course, that Ramon
wouldn't take anything on such occasions, and the risk to his
own career was enormous. But Bob is such a loving and trusting
person that youngsters who work with him become very protective of him and their relationship. Teaching a youngster to care
more about being trusted than about what he can steal is no
small accomplishment, and it is one of Bob's very special contributions to our program.

Our society frowns on risk-taking and severely punishes the
risk-taker who miscalculates. Yet the nature of the problems we
face at The DOME Project and the paucity of resources we have
to combat them forces us to take risks all the time. Sometimes
these risks entail the possibility of grave physical injury. Building the dome involved using power tools, working on scaffolding, and participating in many activities the law specifically pro-
hibits youngsters the age of our dome-builders from doing on
a well-supervised, professional construction site. These same
youngsters may spend their free time dangling precariously
between subway cars or leaping from rooftop to rooftop, but
once we organize them into some type of activity, we become
responsible for their safety.

Recently a New York jury awarded a youngster $1.25 million
in a suit against his high school baseball coach and the Board
of Education. The boy had been hit in the head with a baseball
while sliding into home plate, and his coach was held liable for
not having taught him how to slide so as to avoid injury in that
particular situation. How would a jury have ruled if one of the

dome-builders had slipped off the wet scaffold or, worse yet, if Ted hadn't stopped Lee's axe in time? What insurance company would be so unmindful of its own interests as to insure a group of unskilled young men who planned to build a huge dome on the side of a mountain with two dozen wild teenagers wielding dangerous instruments?

A society in which everyone sues his neighbor on the slightest pretext, as Americans do now, seems certain to accomplish three things: reduce everyone's sense of adventure and willingness to take risks, impoverish all services to a lowest common denominator of mediocrity or worse, and enrich a large number of law firms and insurance companies. We have become a nation of timid souls, afraid even to offer first aid to a wounded neighbor for fear he will recover and sue us for improper treatment. Perhaps the most profound effect on our nation has been the sense so many of us share that — whether we speak of medicine or education or government — most people seem more intent on avoiding or covering up malpractice than on developing excellence in the practice of human services.

The DOME Project, by working with youngsters whom no one else wants to serve, has more leeway in which to operate than most service organizations. The school system expects our students to fail, so it does not really hold us accountable for their performance. The rest of society cares only that these youngsters remain invisible and don't surface from the anonymity of statistics to become individual problems. Their own parents are often so demoralized and fed up that they are willing to let us try almost anything we think might work. And even the youngsters themselves are so convinced they will fail that they don't expect much from us as teachers.

*

Ramon had so much ground to cover that we should probably have kept him in junior high school for four or five years, just trying to teach him how to read and write. Preparing him adequately for high school in the two years we had to work with him was simply not feasible. But we couldn't see holding him back indefinitely. That would only have humiliated him further and confirmed his suspicions that there was something wrong with him. We felt we had to send Ramon, ready or not, on to West Side High School. To most youngsters such a change merely means moving along in the natural flow. To Ramon it meant leaving the only environment in which he had experienced success and exposing himself to a new and threatening challenge.

RAMON: Although I felt I had learned a lot at The DOME, still, just the words *high school* sounded to me like something I couldn't possibly be ready for. Everybody told me not to worry, but I couldn't help it. I was afraid I was gonna fail again.

West Side High turned out to be a nice place. The teachers all encouraged me a lot. The trouble was if you learned even a little there, everybody acted as if you had learned a lot. I had gotten used to The DOME, where everybody expected a lot from me. I began to think some of these teachers had never seen somebody proud before.

In fact, the teachers at West Side High were so delighted to find such a cooperative and hard-working student that they went out of their way to praise his every accomplishment. Despite his serious concern about their lack of demanding standards, Ramon thrived at the school and proudly displayed a report card full of excellent grades. He continued to work with Bob after school and always came down to see us or get help with his school assignments when Bob had nothing for him to do.

The summer after Ramon's freshman year, his mother decided to return to Puerto Rico. Her health was failing, and she had never been happy in New York. The older children could fend for themselves, and she would take the younger ones with her. Only Ramon presented a problem. At fifteen he was too young to look after himself. He was very close to his mother, and the thought of being separated from her made tears well up in his eyes. On the other hand, he couldn't face the idea of starting all over again just when everything seemed to be going so well. He knew if he returned to Puerto Rico he would be put back several grades until he learned to read and write Spanish, and he figured he would probably get discouraged and drop out before that happened.

Shigemi had just moved into an apartment near The DOME Project. He had enjoyed an excellent relationship with Ramon while teaching in the class and readily offered to let him move in. Ramon convinced his mother he really wanted to stay and began transferring his few meager belongings to Shigemi's apartment. Finally, standing in the airport lounge with her two overdressed children amid bursting suitcases and boxes secured with twine, Ramon's mother, her face puffy from crying, confided her son to our care.

A year at West Side High had apparently done much to bolster Ramon's confidence. As his sophomore year approached, he began to worry that the courses offered him wouldn't be demanding enough to help him make the kind of progress he felt he needed to catch up to his peers. I consulted an old friend who was teaching in a remedial program at Queens College, and he arranged for me to meet the program's director. She was receptive to the idea of having Ramon, Ernesto, Isaac, and Michael audit classes so long as we made prior arrangements with the teachers. Our next step was to get West Side High to agree to award credit for the work these youngsters would do at Queens, and that was easily arranged through their independent study program.

Attending Queens College presented a real challenge for Ramon. Only three years earlier he had been afraid to go to the store by himself. Now he was living with Shigemi, traveling by train and bus to another borough to attend class with college students. He chose three courses: English, algebra, and political science. He had to do all the work required of the other students and take all the same exams. On top of this course load he held a job in the evening with a film distribution firm so he could pay his food bill and travel expenses to and from school.

Before the first semester ended, familiar behavior patterns began to reappear in our students. Ernesto became more interested in the social life at Queens than the academic program. Isaac began missing classes and falling behind in his work, but he insisted he could catch up in time to pass all his courses. Michael kept commenting on how easy his classes were, but we could see that he hadn't completed many of the assignments and didn't understand many of the concepts central to the courses he was taking. Only Ramon kept plugging away without trying to cut corners or make excuses. Shigemi reported frequently studying with Ramon until one or two in the morning, and Ramon had to be on the train by six-thirty most mornings in order to get to his first class on time.

Everyone managed to pass at least one course the first semester. Ramon had to repeat English, but he did so well in algebra that his teacher moved him ahead to a more advanced section. The second semester he got the third highest mark in his class on the math final. So great was his satisfaction as he showed his exam paper around The DOME that I feared his grin might permanently damage his cheeks.

That June (1976) an officer of All Angels' Church, where our program was located, offered to help Ramon get a summer job in the' mail room of the First Boston Corporation, a major investment bank on Wall Street. Before the first week was out, Ramon was being asked to put in overtime and handle jobs normally reserved for more experienced employees. With each new experience he was gaining confidence in himself and demystifying another part of the world that had held such terror for him only a few years earlier.

Ramon's next move required another quantum leap of faith on his part, on mine, and on that of the admissions committee of a selective independent boarding school, Lawrence Academy, located in suburban Groton, Massachusetts. The previous year Lawrence Academy had accepted a DOME student on full scholarship and had been sufficiently pleased with his performance to make another opening available to us. It is hard to imagine a more unlikely candidate for admission to a prep school than Ramon, but I felt there were many good reasons to try to get him in: The school would take care of his room and board; he wouldn't have to travel three hours each day to get to and from school; and he wouldn't need an after-school job. He could devote all his energy to studying, and he would also have the facilities available for extracurricular clubs or sports.

The academic program at Lawrence Academy is tough, and we knew Ramon was not adequately prepared. We also knew he was impatient to learn and would put everything he had into trying to succeed. Sending him to Lawrence was a gigantic risk, but we knew of no one who had done more to deserve the chance to get a quality education.

RAMON: The first year at Lawrence was the hardest of my whole life. First of all, I was completely on my own in a strange place. The courses were all about things I had never heard of before. At first I thought, *I'll never be able to do this,* and I started to get discouraged. But I knew a lot of people were counting on me, and I didn't want to let them down, so I just kept trying harder. After a while, some of it began to get a little easier, but I can't say any of it really became a snap. Still, I learned more than I ever did in my life, that's for sure.

Ramon made some remarkable advances that year. He had to repeat a particularly demanding English grammar and fundamentals course, but he passed everything else. He took a Spanish course and learned to read and write his native language, making it possible for him to write directly to his mother without having his letters translated by someone else. He wrote a twelve-page term paper for social studies on the French monarch Louis XIV, typing it one letter at a time. His reading speed improved enough so he could handle the routine chapter-a-night assignments that were handed out, and he learned to voice his opinions in class.

That summer Ramon again worked for First Boston. But by the time he was to return to Lawrence Academy in the fall of 1978, something was wrong. He told me he didn't feel ready to go back, but I was so used to Ramon's nervous griping, dating back five years to his tension headaches, that I shrugged off his remarks from force of habit. Not long afterward, however, I began getting reports from the school that Ramon was sleeping through quizzes and failing to hand in papers. When he came to stay with my family at Thanksgiving, it was apparent something was seriously wrong.

> RAMON: I still don't really know what happened. I just couldn't get myself up for the work. I knew I could do it if I really tried, but I couldn't seem to make myself try harder the way I always had before. As the kids up there say, I sort of bummed out.
>
> When I began falling behind, I got more and more down on myself. I never gave up on anything before in my life, but that's what happened. People tried to talk to me about it, but it didn't do any good.
>
> By Christmastime I just couldn't go back to school. I knew it would hurt a lot of people, but I couldn't help it. I felt like I was going crazy.

Ramon was experiencing a severe form of adolescent depression that seems to affect almost all our youngsters. Their childhoods, largely devoid of recognition and accomplishment, leave them vulnerable to acute crises of self-confidence whenever problems start to mount. Instead of trying to overcome those problems one at a time, the youngsters become almost completely absorbed in a kind of crippling self-pity. They begin excusing their weaknesses rather than working to overcome them.

Ramon's depression was particularly serious because it took the form of regression to a state of mind he had struggled so hard to overcome. I began to worry that I had made a serious mistake in pushing him so hard. My fears were compounded by the discovery that he had started drinking. Ramon had never indulged in the escapist crutches so many other youngsters had used to avoid confronting their own destinies, and I was horrified to think we might have saved Ramon from the frying pan only to watch him be consumed by the fire.

Ramon moved back to New York and went to work full time in the mail room at First Boston. I tried to get him to go back to school, and he did sign up for classes at West Side High. He worked an evening shift so he was free to attend classes during the day, but he just didn't have the will to push himself. The first semester he didn't earn a single credit.

Six months later Ramon found an apartment in our neighborhood. About the same time, one of our youngsters, Peter, was thrown out of his home. We could have tried to force his parents to take Peter back, but the family history indicated that the same situation would only recur, and the period in between would be torture for the youngster. Remembering how Shigemi had taken Ramon in years before when he needed a place to live, we asked Ramon if he would look after Peter until we found him a more suitable and permanent home. I had never asked Ramon for a favor before, but this time I really needed his help.

Perhaps having Peter stay with him reminded Ramon of how far he had come since he was Peter's age. Maybe just accepting responsibility for someone else in worse shape helped take his mind off his own problems. Whatever the answer, Ramon suddenly seemed to perk up. After almost a year of desultory attendance and poor performance at West Side High, he suddenly set out in earnest to get his diploma. He was twenty years old, holding down a full-time job, and looking after a thirteen-year-old boy he hardly knew, yet he managed to struggle through a full course load and pass every subject.

In June of 1980, seven years after he came to us as an illiterate and frightened youngster, Ramon earned his high school diploma. He was one of a handful of students in his school to pass the required citywide competency tests in math, English, and social studies the first time around. He had learned to read fluently and write correctly. He even made a speech at his graduation ceremony, thanking everyone for standing by him when even he had lost faith in himself. For a graduation present we had Ramon's diploma framed, but instead of hanging it on his wall he sent it to his mother in Puerto Rico. He was the first member of his family to earn a diploma, and he hoped it would inspire his younger brother and sister to stay in school and earn theirs as well.

Were it not for Ramon's willingness to trust in us, his courage, determination, and will to take risks, he might still be unskilled and apprehensive. Had The DOME Project not given Ramon the initial boost and then persisted with him over seven difficult years, he might have fallen prey to the depression that was always hovering over him like a vulture, waiting for him to falter. As it was, we weathered a number of crises together, and Ramon came out a winner. He has a good job, a nice apartment, and the respect of everyone who knows him.

Ramon was always a wonderful youngster. We didn't teach him the values that set him apart as a person of great moral integrity. His mother did. Nor did we instill in him his great tenacity or marvelous sense of humor. We did, however, show him that knowledge was not a secret treasure nor learning a mysterious rite from which he had been arbitrarily excluded. We helped him discover that, far from being brain-damaged, he could accomplish as much as he had the courage to attempt. In a society that often succeeds in reducing such youngsters as Ramon to a state of permanent dependency, that seems to me a significant accomplishment.

Chapter Nine

Failures of Our Own

... the most dangerous creation of any society is that man who
has nothing to lose.

JAMES BALDWIN
The Fire Next Time

WHEN LUTHER SEABROOK offered me the chance to work in
my own way with a few youngsters in February 1973, I never
suspected I would be building a dome the following summer or
struggling eight years later to get Ramon to complete his high
school education. In fact, I saw the job as a temporary position,
probably lasting no more than five months, that would allow me
to try something interesting while I decided what I really wanted
to do.

The program grew in what I like to think of as an organic
fashion. As the needs of the youngsters in the class became
apparent, I — alone at first and then with those friends who
came to work with me — tried to create appropriate responses.
Some of those responses, like building the dome, were dramatic
and involved great physical risks; others, like sticking with a
youngster through a long and complex developmental cycle,
were tedious and involved substantial psychological gambles.
Not all the risks paid off, but they were generally worth taking.

At least we could feel that our successes and our failures were our own. When things went wrong, we generally had no one to blame but ourselves.

I had developed a crazy way to run a program. Building on the evident needs of our youngsters guaranteed a fluid and responsive operation but made it virtually impossible to plan ahead or develop a budget. Having different friends work for a semester or two provided plenty of fresh ideas and was certainly better than having no one to help, but as the program expanded and became increasingly complex, I began to feel the need for more consistent support.

By September 1974, the dome was up and the class had grown from five to a dozen students. Arthur and Shigemi had both taught with me for a semester and were now followed by Bobby, a young man who had been one of the first participants I had come to know well at the Youth Center. I had subsequently helped him get into my former college, Hamilton, from which he took a semester's leave to work in the classroom. The Youth Center lent me a second assistant, Chris, a seventeen-year-old fresh out of West Side High School.

*

A typical day that autumn began at 8:00 A.M., when I would pick up the breakfast from I.S. 44 and carry it over to the church basement, where Bobby and Chris would meet me. Our dozen students would drift in for class between 8:30 and 10:00 in various states of readiness, ranging from enthusiasm to rage. We sorely missed Miriam, who had decided to seek a master's degree in social work at Hunter College. Her maternal presence had certainly helped create a calmer and softer tone in the classroom.

After lunch Ernesto, Isaac, Michael, Lee, and four other West Side High students who had either been in our class or helped build the dome arrived for a special class. We had worked out a half-day arrangement with West Side High in order to keep them motivated and in constant touch with our program. While Bobby and Chris worked with our junior high school students, I taught literature and writing to the older boys.

At 3:00 P.M. a further influx of students from I.S. 44 and nearby high schools arrived to participate in a new project. We had rented a storefront up the block from the church basement that housed our program and spent three months renovating it. After visiting schools and youth programs to recruit exhibitors, we opened a student-run gift and craft boutique called the Student Design Center. Every item in the shop was made by youngsters. We sold their work on a commission basis, taking only the minimum percentage we felt we needed to maintain the store. We had a student manager, student bookkeeper, student salesclerks, and student cashiers.

We closed the shop at 7:00 P.M. each weekday evening and tried to keep it open Saturdays too. Since we spent many evening hours visiting parents, writing proposals for new funding, or trying to resolve crises for our youngsters and their families, we didn't have much time for ourselves. Bobby and Chris were both young and single and had no other responsibilities weighing on them. I had a six-month-old child who kept waking up during the night and a wife who wondered if I would ever consent to anything resembling a normal family life. I realized I was spreading myself too thin, but there was little I could do once I had committed myself to all those activities except grit my teeth and try to make it through the school year.

While I was trying to figure out how to stretch the day so I could find more time for Hannele and Mikko, my father died, leaving my mother alone and me with a terrible sense of loss. Dad was the kind of man who kept many of his thoughts and feelings to himself, but he was extremely loving and always there when his family needed him. He had been a great source of strength to me and the one person to whom I could turn confidently for advice or encouragement when I needed it. His judgment was reliable, his values fair and firm, and his behavior honorable. Without him I would have to rely increasingly on my own inner resources.

As if these personal difficulties were not enough to weigh me down, the program was falling apart. To begin with, the class was a catastrophe. I had foolishly allowed I.S. 44 to foist on me a large number of students who had no interest in attending any program. They agreed to my contract only because our class seemed like the least unpleasant alternative available. Many of the youngsters were already immersed in a criminal lifestyle of incredible complexity. Three of them, each not yet fifteen and standing barely five feet tall, had been arrested more than thirty times. Some of our students openly bragged of muggings and robberies in which they had participated and the various weapons to which they had access.

Most schools present themselves primarily as institutions designed to transfer to their students a certain body of skills and information. We have always treated The DOME Project as a vehicle for a much more comprehensive kind of personal and social development. We try to help our youngsters become happy, healthy adults with positive social values and the opportunity to lead productive lives. We want them to have the same kinds of options most parents wish for their children. How they exercise those options is ultimately their choice, but at least we try to convince them there are real choices to be made and real reasons to choose one kind of life over another.

We work hard to reinforce family ties, not replace or diminish them. By including parents and siblings in activities and decision making, we create a kind of extended family that gives each youngster a sense of belonging to a powerful and protective clan. Youth gangs often perform a similar function in neighborhoods where there is no other effective intermediary between the struggling nuclear family and society at large.

Most adolescents think they know what they want, and they are often able to resist or subvert whatever plans others may make for them. We offer youngsters school and work incentives, powerful role models, and a protective and nourishing environment. We create an extended family and positive peer associations in an attempt to alter or limit certain kinds of behavior. In the end, however, our success or failure will be determined by the extent to which the youngsters choose to participate.

The students we ended up with in 1974–75, with the lone exception of Ramon, showed little inclination to take advantage of what we had to offer. I am not certain why. Part of the answer may lie in the concept of balance. The forces of chaos in that class may simply have outweighed all the forces of order we could generate. A few especially hardened youngsters mixed in with a group open to change can function in a program such as ours. That year, as it turned out, we had too many youngsters who already believed the die had been cast for them. They had all been held back in junior high school the maximum number of times allowable and knew they would be kicked upstairs to high school at year's end no matter how much or how little progress they made. Most of them had acquired a sense of importance and identity through their criminal activities. They were not about to trade in this hard-won status for a pat on the head and a little praise from us.

Partly because many of my students were on probation from family court, I could get them to attend class regularly, but the quality of daily life in the classroom was unbearable. A more experienced staff would have had a tough time with this lot, but Bobby, Chris, and I were simply overwhelmed, and we paid a heavy price. By the time Bobby left to return to college in January, I was at the end of my rope. I needed help desperately, and the person I turned to was Ted.

Ted had left the day-care center a few months earlier and had not yet taken another job. While he wouldn't commit himself to anything more than helping me through the school year, just his presence and maturity took much of the pressure off me. Ted knew I was having a hard time, but I think he was genuinely shocked when he first witnessed the attitudes and behavior of some of my students at first hand.

TED: I couldn't believe what I found in the class. The first thing those kids would do every morning was hunker down and hash over all the horror stories of what had happened the night before. They told the most incredibly gory tales of violence and brutality, of knifings and stompings and bloodshed. Their total fascination — just the looks on their faces — was awful. The tension in the room was unbelievable. There was a constant sense that from nowhere, for no particular reason, an explosion would occur.

Ted insists he took the job at The DOME because it was the best offer he had at the time, but I know better. He agreed to do it, against all his instincts for self-preservation, because I was in trouble.

The bright spot for me in each day was when our West Side High students came down for their special class. The course I designed for them was unreasonably ambitious, considering their very modest reading skills, but knowing the generally unpalatable remedial assignments they got in school I wanted to expose them to challenging and exciting works. First we read short stories by O. Henry, passages from Genesis, and poems by Robert Frost, Langston Hughes, and e.e. cummings. Then I decided to introduce my students to *Oedipus the King*.

Reading Sophocles with Lee, Michael, Isaac, Ernesto, Julio, and a few others was a fascinating experience. It took us nearly two hours to read the first twenty-five lines. The vocabulary, the syntax, the setting were all so strange and to them. None of them had any idea where Greece was nor had any of them ever attended a live theater performance.

The following day we reread the same lines in just ten minutes and went on to complete two more pages before stopping. My students could now identify Thebes and Zeus and knew the meanings of *suppliant* and *oracle,* and they didn't complain quite so vehemently when I stopped to explain some details I felt were important.

By the third day, everyone had become deeply involved in the plot, especially Ernesto, who was ready to come to blows with anyone who challenged his right to read the part of Oedipus. They called Creon "Crayon" and Tiresias "Tire-ass," but they read the play with an intensity I suspect the ancient Greeks would have appreciated, shouting out their discoveries like children in a puppet theater warning the woodsman to beware of the wolf lurking behind the tree. I'm not sure how much they learned about classical Greek drama, but I never saw a group of students enjoy a play more thoroughly. We finished the whole play and then went back and reread it to get a feel for how it would sound without all the interruptions. I doubt whether any of those youngsters ever went on to read a second Greek tragedy, but I could derive some satisfaction from knowing they at least had learned the classical, literary derivation of the term *motherfucker*.

As much as I enjoyed working with my former students, their presence in the program contributed greatly to our problems. We had made them feel The DOME Project was an extension of their home and family, and then we had brought in a new group of students. The veterans reacted with the same petulant jealousy parents are warned to expect from their children when they bring a new baby home from the hospital. At first they tried to take out their anger on the new students, picking fights with them on the slightest pretext. When we put a stop to that, they gradually turned their resentment against the staff.

They knew they were behaving badly, and often felt guilty, but their feelings were hurt and they couldn't stand it. They started coming to The DOME high, partly to soften their feelings of guilt and anger and partly to embolden themselves for whatever confrontation might arise. They also got high to torment me, knowing how deeply I felt drug abuse was a sign of disrespect for our program and for themselves. I would send them home whenever I saw they were high, but some were better at concealing the condition than others. It became a kind of extremely unpleasant game they would play with me to see whether I could tell who had been smoking reefer and who had not.

I had been training these youngsters to become leaders in our program. They had helped define the range and character of activities we provided. Now they were undermining not only my authority but the major premises of cooperation and shared objectives upon which we had built the program. We had gone so far as to establish a leadership council empowered to make some important decisions, but the council was unable to provide any constructive leadership in this instance because the council members were among the worst offenders.

Tension mounted day by day. Ted warned me we were heading for some kind of explosion. I agreed but couldn't figure out what to do to head it off. I kept trying to talk to the youngsters who were most obviously unhappy, but nothing I said seemed to help.

One day I caught Lee smoking a joint in the stairwell of the church. Lee had almost killed someone with an axe at the dome site, and we had kept him in the program. He had walked out of high school, and we had taken him into our class. We had gotten him into West Side High, found him jobs, and befriended him in many ways. Despite these efforts, or perhaps because of them, Lee was one of those most disoriented by the arrival of the younger students.

I asked Lee to leave the building, but he just stood there as if he hadn't even heard me. I asked him again, more forcefully this time. Instead of leaving he walked into the classroom and sat down. Had I been a little less tired and in a better frame of mind, I probably would have given him a few minutes to find some way to leave gracefully. I was too upset, however, to respond rationally. I bolted after him, raised my voice, and ordered him to leave immediately. I could see the anger welling up in him, but my own fury was equally great.

Our confrontation had become the center of attention. The other youngsters were drawn to us like sharks toward the smell of blood. Lee was strong, strong enough so that I didn't look forward to grappling with him, but I was determined to move him out. As I started toward him, I didn't notice Lee taking a razor-sharp box cutter from his pocket. As I got close enough to put my hand on him, Lee stood up and suddenly lunged toward me. I grabbed him and pinned his arms, but he was still able to draw the blade across my back. Fortunately I was wearing a thick sweater. The point left only a long, ugly scratch from one shoulder blade to the small of my back. After I finally got Lee out to the street and on his way home, though, I realized I was trembling and horribly afraid.

The incident disturbed me deeply. I knew that Lee genuinely cared for me, but he had put himself, with my assistance, in a situation in which only the slightest alteration in circumstances might have resulted in his killing me. Something was dreadfully wrong with the direction the program was taking. If I didn't do something about it, the participants in the next incident might not escape so lightly.

Meanwhile, our younger students were watching carefully everything that was happening. Unlike the older program participants, they had no long-standing relationships to bind them to the staff. We had no way of predicting what they might do in any given situation. Some of them had begun to show some interest in improving their reading and writing skills or in getting into a high school in which they might have a chance to succeed, but we had done very little to change their fascination for and involvement in antisocial behavior.

TED: There was an atmosphere of violence that followed some of those kids wherever they went. It culminated in their thinking they could attack people without having to face any serious consequences. We had no stomach for hitting kids, yet some of them felt you weren't serious unless you were willing to back up your demands physically. In what way does belting a kid teach him anything you can use to rebuild a viable relationship? It may possibly have some deterrent effect on others, but you want a kid who did something wrong to learn his lesson, not be the lesson.

Nevertheless I realized by the end of the year that some of the most disturbed kids in the class, youngsters who probably didn't belong there in the first place, loved some of the people in the program. The relationships they established with us may have been the only decent ones they ever had in their lives.

Like Ted, I worried about these youngsters and how to reach them, and I particularly worried about Lee. I knew I couldn't allow him back in the program without communicating to everyone else my tolerance of his behavior. Yet I had never banished anyone before. Wasn't I, as Ted suggested, making him the lesson instead of teaching it to him? I knew throwing him out of the program was equivalent to pushing him out on the street. How would he survive?

LEE: I always thought I must be here for a purpose, but I couldn't find out why. I used to ask myself, *Why was I born?* Things like that.

I used to walk through the streets and wonder why I didn't have nobody walkin' with me, nobody to talk to. Other people always seemed to have family with them, but my family always seemed to be comin' down on me. I guess I felt more alone than most other kids.

When I be doin' somethin' bad, I wouldn't be thinkin' about what could happen later. I'd just be thinkin' where to run.

Afterwards, though, I'd feel bad inside, like I shouldn't have did that. I'd think, *Those people be out hustlin' at they jobs, and I'm over here takin' the money they work for.* I'd be thinking, *What's gonna happen to me if I keep doing stuff like this?*

In that pathetic voice I hear echoes of Michael describing conditions in the Vernon Hotel, Ernesto longing for some encouragement from his father, and Ramon hoping that some day he would have some skill or knowledge with which to make a useful place for himself in the world. None of these youngsters wanted charity or sympathy. They wanted a chance to be productive. They wanted to know what other people knew, do what other people did, and enjoy the kinds of relationships other people seemed to enjoy. To the extent their circumstances permitted, they were willing to work for those opportunities.

Our society, however, seems to begrudge these young people the room and time they need to grow. Many do not get the love and recognition essential to the development of a healthy personality. They grow up fearing they will never be valued, a worry they share with all adolescents to a certain extent, but the circumstances of their lives reinforce the sense that they have nothing to gain and, therefore, nothing to lose.

We all want recognition. If we can't attain it through talent or hard work, we may seek other routes. In an interview in *The New Yorker,* a New York City police officer who was laid off because of budget cuts was asked how he would support his family once his unemployment benefits ran out. He responded that he fully expected to get his job back, but if he didn't, he added, "At least I know how to use a gun." I have heard similar sentiments, time and again, from young people who see their hopes and dreams of making it in legitimate ways destroyed by a society that doesn't value their potential contribution.

Every youngster wants to grow up to be a star, but the mass of nonwhite urban adolescents are like extras milling around a set the producers have abandoned. They have no script, no role, and the filming has been moved to a different location. There can be little argument about the cost to everyone, from mugger to victim, from taxpayer to welfare recipient, of a socioeconomic system that allows so substantial a portion of its populace, and particularly its youth, to become extraneous.

Youngsters often turn to delinquent behavior for the simple but frightening reason that they don't see any alternative for themselves. They fail at school, although our schools must surely share some of the blame. They cannot find work, for there is no work for them to do. They are irresponsible but at least in part because they lack a role to play in our society that might carry with it some responsibility and teach them something about being response-able.

It is hard for anyone, let alone confused adolescents, to maintain a fine sense of moral balance when they believe neither they nor their actions matter to anyone. These youngsters develop instead an opportunistic set of values that reflects both the moral fluidity of society and their lack of a stable position in it. I don't mean to suggest these youngsters have no principles to which they adhere, for that is not the case. Their standards for ethical judgment, however, are so different from those I derived from my middle-class upbringing that I often have to remind myself not to assume I know what these youngsters are thinking or what basis they may use for making decisions.

At the end of the 1974–75 school year I gave a little essay assignment to my class. The surprising response I got may help illustrate my point. I asked my junior high school students to comment on one of the aphorisms my father used to trot out whenever I began to feel sorry for myself: "I cried because I had no shoes until I met a man who had no feet." I assigned this topic to ten students in a setting where they could not consult with each other. I wanted to see how well each one could deal with the simple sentiment transmitted by the single sentence. The results really shocked me. Two or three students wrote about feeling sorry for themselves until they saw someone worse off, but the rest of the papers all conveyed a different message: "This means I cried because I had no shoes and my feet was cold and sore. Then I met a man who had no feet. I thought, *He don't need his shoes,* so I took them. After that my feet felt better."

Many of the youngsters with whom I work are so wrapped up in their own needs that they cannot see or relate to the needs of others. They steal, as Lee had done, simply because they don't have something they want and see someone else who has it. To them, their needs supersede the needs of everyone else. The same is, in one way or another, true of us all, but most of us respond to other constraints upon our behavior. Lee told me he felt bad about robbing a working man because he knew he was stealing not just a wallet but days or weeks of that man's labor, yet he did it just the same.

I stayed in touch with Lee after I forced him to leave The DOME. He carried crumpled in his wallet the letter I wrote him a few days after he tried to stab me. I tried to encourage him to stay in school, and I helped find him jobs when he dropped out. I also got him lawyers and appeared with him in court. None of it really helped, at least not to the point where it might have enabled him to hold himself together. Lee had no anchor. Rejection by his father and hatred of his stepfather had left him lonely and bitter. Alcohol and drugs had robbed him of his equilibrium. He became a person who felt he had nothing to live for.

Lee was not the only youngster we lost. During the years I have worked at The DOME Project, we have lost students to drugs, jail, and the cemetery. I have seen youngsters run away and waste away. We did what we could, but often we were powerless to help. There is only so much a small program can do to counteract pressures exerted by the rest of society.

Some failures are harder to endure than others, but the failure to help a child who is calling out to you is the hardest of all. I harden my heart. I say I did everything I could. I remind myself of all those still looking to our program for guidance and support. But sometimes I cannot screen out the pain. Then I think of Lee and remember the tone of panic in his voice as he ran away from his mother and me the last time we were in court together, and I hope he has found someone who can help him more than I did.

PART THREE

ORDINARY YOUNGSTERS, DEFORMING CIRCUMSTANCES

Chapter Ten

Carlos: From Playing Hooky to Great Expectations

"We changed back again, and yet again, and it was now too late and too far to go back, and I went on. And the mists had all solemnly risen now, and the world lay spread before me."

CHARLES DICKENS
Great Expectations

POVERTY ALONE does not necessarily constitute a deforming circumstance in the lives of children. It may not make life any easier, but there is ample literature testifying to the possibility of poor children having fulfilling lives. The poverty to which Michael was subjected in the slums and welfare hotels of his childhood and which Lee experienced as a young man who never had any of the things he wanted was so bleak and oppressive that it distorted their development. They grew like saplings in rocky soil deprived of proper nourishment so that their personalities became gnarled and twisted like coastal pines. Ramon, on the other hand, experienced a childhood of material deprivation that was nevertheless rich in human interaction. He grew up with the ability to give as well as take and pursue what is right instead of only what is self-serving.

While the youngsters in our program tend to be louder, more

physical in their relationships and more destructive of property than the youngsters with whom I grew up in my tiny suburban hometown, they are also more generous, loyal, and protective of one another. They are no more cruel than we were as children, although they sometimes express that cruelty differently. While differing circumstances and environments influence youngsters to grow and develop in different ways, most young people seem to be able to survive all but the most destructive experiences intact.

Surviving, however, is a poor substitute for enjoying a full and rewarding life. As many people have learned the hard way, growing older is not the same as growing up. Many of the young people with whom we work risk growing to adulthood without any understanding of how they might exert some control over the circumstances shaping their lives. Like Isaac, they learn to bend under pressure without breaking or avoid their problems for as long as possible and then try to shrug off the consequences. Such a strategy has probably saved Isaac from becoming bitter and destructive like Lee, but it has also ensured his continued powerlessness. He is still a delightful person but probably unemployable for any extended period and much too susceptible to unrealistic spurts of optimism and fits of depression.

The waste of human potential in youngsters like Isaac is enormous. It is even more tragic and needless in the case of someone like Carlos, a young man I met soon after I began working at the Youth Center. As an eleven-year-old he had managed to win a starting spot at second base on the Youth Center's team for fourteen- to sixteen-year-olds. Carlos was so small that the letters on his shirt disappeared into his pants and his cap kept slipping down over his eyes when he would bend to scoop up a ground ball, yet he could play better than most of the bigger boys. Nothing ever got past him at second, and he protected his tiny strike zone tenaciously.

When Carlos came to us for help he was seventeen and supposedly entering his senior year at a vocational high school specializing in printing trades. He was bright, a good athlete, well liked by everyone, had a steady girlfriend, and generally seemed to be on top of the world. I thought he might want advice on selecting a college or finding a good summer job and was surprised to learn he needed help with a much more serious problem. He told me he barely had a 60 percent average for the four years he had been attending high school. He had been truant most of the previous year, failed all his courses, and now would not graduate on schedule. What compounded Carlos's problem was that he had managed to conceal his malingering from his parents. They thought he was doing well and had already begun making plans, although it was only October, to bring his grandparents up from Puerto Rico for the graduation. Carlos didn't have the nerve to tell them the truth, but he couldn't see any way to forestall the awful revelation that would come by graduation time, if not before.

Carlos had always been a good boy. Had he been white and grown up in the same Westchester community as I, he undoubtedly would have been a class officer or student council president. He had that kind of charisma. He probably would not have been a top scholar, but he would have maintained a decent average and been accepted at several respectable colleges. He might have drunk some beer and smoked some pot, but he wouldn't have cut school for an entire year. I am not suggesting that suburban school systems don't have their problems, but I doubt many of them have broken down to the point where a youngster with Carlos's potential can simply disappear from school for a year without his parents even knowing about his truancy.

Hernando, Carlos's father, is a shoemaker who grew up in a rural mountain village in Puerto Rico. His own father died when he was quite young. Although he had completed only a few years of rudimentary schooling, Hernando had to leave home and apprentice himself to a cobbler who said he was willing to teach him the trade. The man exploited Hernando unscrupulously, demanding long hours of hard labor without making any serious attempts to teach him anything. Nevertheless, Hernando was observant and diligent, and after a few years felt he knew enough to run off to San Juan, where he got a job as an assistant in a shoe repair shop. Lonely and overworked, he married while still a teenager and began raising a family.

HERNANDO: Before thirty I have five children, ages from eleven year to one year. Carlos is the one in the middle. I was working fourteen hours a day, six days a week, sometimes even Sundays, and still I don't make enough to eat good, just to survive.

My wife first put the idea to me to come to the States. At first I was afraid I couldn't make it. I couldn't speak not even one word of English. But I agree to try because I see the chance I can give my family a better life. I had to make a lot of sacrifice, but thanks God I did it. I really appreciate what this country been for us.

My wife and me come with the idea to work and make ourselves better. I don't have an education, but I know to work hard. I still work eleven hours a day, and I don't need no welfare. I would like to go to school to learn good English, but I have no time. When I come home at night, I want to be with my family. Every English I know, I have to learn it from customer in the shoe shop.

My boys, sometimes they think they know better than me because they speak better and go to school. But I try to explain them, when they was little I was already in the street and I know what was happening. I see so many things, and that's why I scared for them.

Certainly there was plenty to be scared of in the neighborhood around the decrepit tenement in which Hernando's family lived. The drug traffic was fierce. Every little store had a gambling room in the back; I once counted twenty-six numbers parlors in a six-block stretch of avenue. There were frequent gang fights, with shootings sometimes taking place around school buildings or subway stations. Yet Hernando succeeded in protecting his family, and Carlos remembers his childhood as a happy time.

As vigilant as Hernando was, however, and as alert to the dangers of the street, he was not sufficiently familiar with the complex New York City school system to guide his children skillfully through its maze of choices and limitations. There was nothing in Hernando's background to suggest to him that he would have to evaluate critically every decision by the professionals to whom he entrusted his children's education. Like so many people with little formal education, he had an exaggerated sense both of his own inadequacy and of the wisdom and skill of people possessing college diplomas. He would never have felt comfortable challenging the views of a teacher or guidance counselor.

Parents everywhere must do exactly that, however, to protect the interests of their children. Whether in the finest institution or the worst, teachers and administrators will make some decisions for the convenience of the institution instead of in the best interests of the child. In this respect The DOME Project is no different from any other school, and we have learned much from parents who have taken us to task over the way we have dealt with or neglected to deal with certain of their children's problems.

One problem parents must watch for carefully is discriminatory grouping of youngsters in ways that limit or determine the kinds of careers and future opportunities available to them later in life. Because youngsters develop at a different pace, both intellectually and emotionally, a school can do irreparable damage to a youngster by tracking him or her at an early age into a program that may prove ultimately inappropriate. People often ask me if my opposition to tracking doesn't conflict with the logic behind a special class such as ours at The DOME Project. In fact, our youngsters display an unusually broad range of skills, interests, and backgrounds. The only quality all of them share is an inability to tolerate or benefit from the other school settings and programs available to them.

The regular elementary and junior high schools in New York City are supposed to perform parallel functions and, with few exceptions, serve the entire range of young people within their catchment area. Before going on to high school, however, youngsters are confronted with a bewildering array of choices. No one automatically moves on to a neighborhood high school, for even the comprehensive high schools are grouped by zones, and youngsters are asked to choose one over the others. In addition to the comprehensive schools, students who can pass the entrance exams may choose from elite schools, educational option schools, vocational schools for those who prefer to learn a trade, and alternative schools geared to the needs of youngsters with diverse learning styles.

The high school one attends can make an enormous difference in the kind of education one gets, and parents who understand the system well can often help their children manipulate it to their own advantage. Preparations can range from compiling portfolios or rehearsing performances to studying for specific entrance exams. I have known parents to hire tutors to help their children study for these exams and put enormous pressure on their children to succeed. The payoffs seem to many people to justify these extraordinary efforts. Youngsters who make it to such elite schools as Stuyvesant High School or the Bronx High School of Science, for example, stand an excellent chance of gaining admission to a top college; youngsters who attend zoned or vocational schools have a good chance of dropping out. While New York public school Chancellor Frank Macchiarola admitted in 1979 that barely half the students entering ninth grade in New York City schools eventually graduate, his figures included all the elite and specialized high schools. Many of the zoned high schools serving the Manhattan district where our program is located graduate only one youngster in four. The other three fall by the wayside.

New York City high school students score an average forty-five points lower on Scholastic Aptitude Tests, both verbal and math, than the national average. Some high schools do an adequate job of preparing a majority of their students, but clearly others do not, and those who end up in the least desirable high schools are generally those who either have no choice or have not exercised that choice intelligently.

Hernando, Carlos's father, had no understanding of these complexities and relied on the junior high school guidance office to help his son make an appropriate choice. Unfortunately, recurring budget cuts have taken a heavy toll on guidance counselors, and the guidance office was, in reality, a single overworked woman who could barely keep up with all the paperwork. She rarely was able to meet even once with most of the students in the school. Carlos ended up making his choice according to criteria that should have had little bearing on so important a decision.

CARLOS: I knew the New York School of Printing was a vocational school, and I knew I didn't want to be a printer. I chose it because a lot of my friends were going there and because it was neither too near my home nor too far away.

I started my freshman year with enthusiasm, but the longer I stayed there, the more certain I became that I didn't want to be a printer. I didn't want to stay there, but I didn't know what to do about it. Instead of trying to transfer I got discouraged, and that's when things really started going wrong.

The summer before my sophomore year I began getting into a lot of arguments at home. After work I would go across town to a park where the best baseball games were. I was supposed to be home by nine, and sometimes we'd still be in the middle of a game. A couple of times Pop came to fetch me and pulled me right off the field in front of all the guys. That really humiliated me.

I was fifteen, and a lot of guys my age could stay out until two or three in the morning. My friends would all tease me about having to be in early, and I hated it. I felt my parents were treating me like a baby.

All parents, sooner or later, have to contend with the argument that, "Johnny's mother lets him do it so why can't I?" The usual reply is, "Because you're not Johnny, and that's the last I want to hear about it!" In a community where most parents have roughly similar standards and values, Johnny's parents can usually be shown to be out of line by citing all the other youngsters who must endure the stricter limits. In New York City, however, there seem to be almost as many standards and norms as there are families.

Carlos predictably didn't get very far trying to buck his father's rules. Increasingly frequent arguments at home added to the depressed feeling he was beginning to have about school. He started cutting classes his sophomore year, occasionally at first and more frequently as he saw he could get away with it.

CARLOS: School was terrible. We had huge classes, and a lot of the kids had worse problems than I did. Everyone would give the teachers such a hard time that eventually most of them would just give up. If a teacher really knew how to control a classroom, we would show him some respect. Otherwise we would take advantage of even the nicest person.

When I first went to high school I never dared to cut even a single class. After a while I started noticing how many guys would come in for attendance and then cut out just before some class they didn't like. Someone was always trying to talk me into going to the park or the movies instead of staying in school. I never had to go, but after a while I got so fed up with school I just gave in. I cut the last period one day, and before long I was playing hooky regularly.

All the school would do when I cut classes was send a little card home to my parents. I found out what day they sent out the cards and would get them from the mailbox before Pop got home from work. That way my parents never knew what was happening.

I felt guilty as hell about what I was doing, but I told myself my parents just didn't understand me at all. I needed some time of my own to be with friends, talk to girls, play ball, discuss my problems, and just goof around. If my parents didn't know what I was doing every minute, they thought I was using dope or stealing things. A lot of the kids I knew were doing those things, but I wasn't, and I didn't think it was fair for them to treat me that way. Pop had a rough life when he was young, and I guess that made him very strict, but to me his ideas were just old-fashioned.

The part of Carlos's story that made no sense to me was that he could cut school for over a year without his family detecting it. Apparently the school absolved itself of all responsibility for trying to get Carlos back into class by mailing little notices. Hernando had no telephone, so someone would have had to make the effort to visit the family to find out why Carlos wasn't attending school, but no one ever did. Perhaps it is not surprising in a school of four or five thousand within a school system of nearly a million that youngsters get lost this way, but it is nonetheless tragic. Here was a bright youngster with tremendous potential, a supportive family willing to cooperate in any way, and a school system unable to inform the family that their son was in trouble.

A friend recently returned from the mountainous region of southern Haiti, where he was inoculating the inhabitants as part of a United Nations program. He showed me a photo of a slender man in his early forties, barefoot, wearing khaki shorts and a plain white shirt, surrounded by two dozen equally barefoot children who appeared to range in age from about nine to eleven. "This teacher," my friend told me, "walked all night through the mountains with his class to see that the children all got their shots." Clearly this man had no trouble identifying with the needs of his students. I don't expect urban teachers to walk all night through mountain wilderness with their students, but is it too much to ask for a short subway ride uptown to try to help a youngster get back on the right track before he is so far behind he can never catch up?

Hernando tried to monitor his children's progress in school. At first he regularly went to school meetings. After a while, though, he got discouraged and felt he was just wasting his time. By the time Carlos reached high school, Hernando stopped going to the schools and relied on the teachers to make the same kind of honest effort to educate his children that he would have made to repair the teachers' shoes.

> HERNANDO: I stopped going to the school to find out how Carlos is doing because I never understand what the teachers saying to me. Anyway, the schools here have so many problems I never see in my country. How can I know what to do?
>
> I have to leave my own school in such a low grade, I cannot help my children in their study. I can't even read the report card. Sometime when they bring it to me, I look at it very serious like I study it, but I can't say if it is good or bad because I don't understand what it means. Maybe I say to my child, "Oh! That's very good," and really it is not good. That probably happen to me a lot of time.

I could hardly blame Hernando for not feeling comfortable visiting his son's school. In order for him to communicate with any of Carlos's teachers, either he or the teacher would have to overcome cultural, class, and language barriers. Since the teachers didn't speak Spanish, Hernando would be the one forced to make the effort.

By the time Carlos sought me out in the fall of 1976, it was clear neither his school nor his parents were going to solve his problems for him. Only Carlos could help himself. Most youngsters in his situation probably would have continued to play hooky and avoided facing the consequences until the very last moment. By coming to me at the beginning of the school year, however, Carlos gave us some time to try to work out a solution to his problem. I wasn't sure how I could help him, but I was willing to try if he would demonstrate a willingness to help himself.

Carlos said he wanted to leave the city and all the problems he associated with it. He asked if I could help him get into some kind of boarding school where he could finish his education. He had no money and a failing average at a public vocational high school not noted for producing scholars. How could I possibly get him into a private school under those circumstances?

I not only had no contacts whatsoever at private schools, I also harbored a firm prejudice against elitist schools that predicated admission on the family's ability to pay. Nevertheless, if private schools were going to exist, I didn't see why some of the youngsters from our program shouldn't have the opportunity to benefit from their small classes and excellent facilities. I began contacting private schools in New England to see if any of them might be even remotely interested in such a poorly prepared candidate.

I knew that getting Carlos into school would be only half the battle. The other half would be making it possible for him to succeed once he got there. Carlos really didn't appear to have adequate skills to handle a prep school curriculum. I told him I expected to see him every day immediately after school, ready to work. I also obtained permission from Hernando for Carlos to study with me instead of helping in the shop. I didn't say anything about why his son had suddenly become so interested in being tutored, but I mentioned Carlos's desire to go away to school. If his father thought I meant college, I hope he will forgive me for this gentle deception.

I started Carlos off reading *Great Expectations.* Reminiscent of my students trying to read *Oedipus,* Carlos needed nearly two hours to read the first page. There is one sentence about the river winding to the sea that must have taken him twenty minutes to unravel. But each day we picked up a little more steam until Carlos could read entire chapters at home. Carlos finished the final third of the book in a week, carrying it with him everywhere and surreptitiously reading it in class whenever his teachers weren't looking.

Two other youngsters who came occasionally for tutoring help, Joe and Edwin, learned about Carlos's desire to go away to school and asked to join our little study group. I told them I didn't even know what I could arrange for Carlos, let alone take on responsibility for all three, but they were welcome to work along with us and see what developed. We read both parts of Shakespeare's *Henry IV,* studied some algebra, and tried to get all their homework done properly and on time.

Carlos made enormous progress, and so did Edwin and Joe. It is extraordinary what difference a little motivation can make in the performance of an underachieving student. Carlos brought in a midyear report card full of grades in the eighties, an average improvement of twenty-five points per class. Edwin and Joe also brought their grades up dramatically, enabling me to think seriously about finding schools for them too.

By early spring I was convinced all three youngsters were intellectually and psychologically ready for a competitive school experience. I began contacting independent schools, almost randomly at first, then following helpful suggestions from admissions directors about other schools. We sent off transcripts, letters of recommendation, and test results from an independent testing center. I also insisted each youngster write an essay comparing his own situation to that of Pip in *Great Expectations* and included these uneven but extremely moving compositions with each one's application.

The first day of Easter vacation the four of us piled into an old Plymouth station wagon someone had donated to the program and headed off to visit three schools that had agreed to interview the boys. All of us shared mixed feelings of excitement and trepidation as we headed into New England. Our anxiety subsided, however, as the visits proceeded smoothly, and the youngsters began to daydream about life as boarding students. A month later the letters arrived. Carlos and Joe were accepted by New Hampton School in central New Hampshire, and Lawrence Academy, where Ramon would go the following year, accepted Edwin. All three letters offered full scholarships. Needless to say, we were delirious. We had succeeded in a venture we realistically never should have attempted. But once the delirium subsided, we realized that the hardest part of the challenge still lay ahead.

CARLOS: When I first got to New Hampton, I panicked. There were only ten kids in each class, and I was used to forty. There was no place to hide.

I had to do all my work because the teacher was sure to call on me in every class, and I didn't want to make a fool of myself. At home everyone thought you were a chump if you did all your schoolwork, but at New Hampton it was the other way around. Sometimes guys from my dorm would come to my room at night to discuss a sociology assignment or read some poems together. It was a completely different world from any I had ever known. Sometimes I'd read something and just get chills from it. I'd want to find one of my friends right away and share it with him.

The school did a lot to make me feel comfortable. I saw that teachers were willing to spend extra time with me, so I wasn't afraid to ask for help when I needed it. They appointed me dorm proctor too, and that made me feel good. They wouldn't have given me that extra responsibility, I thought, unless they were confident I could handle it.

Carlos did well enough in his two years at New Hampton to gain admission to all five colleges to which he applied. Before he decided which one to attend, he came down to New York to discuss his choice with me. He had sent applications to a variety of schools, not knowing how the admissions committees would view his peculiar background. At one extreme was a large and not very demanding university where he could play major college baseball while taking fairly easy classes; at the other was Hamilton College, where he would have to work extremely hard just to stay in. After considerable soul-searching, Carlos chose Hamilton.

CARLOS: I knew I might not make it at Hamilton, but I couldn't see taking second best. If I chickened out, I would never know what I really could do. I had to go for the best education I could get.

No matter what, I knew I would never go back to what I had been before. But I didn't want to forget where I came from either.

Carlos has learned much from his experiences at New Hampton and Hamilton, ranging from how to study to how to fight off bouts of loneliness and depression. Every summer Carlos returns to work with us, coaching neighborhood children in baseball and encouraging them to take their studies seriously. He has become the kind of role model/leader we are trying to develop at The DOME Project. He has become a valuable community resource, and his family is justifiably proud of his achievements.

There must be thousands of youngsters in New York City who resemble Carlos as he was at the start of his senior year in high school. Only a handful, at most, will escape the failure and dejection that would have been Carlos's lot if he hadn't taken the initiative to seek help and had the good fortune to live in a community with a program whose staff members were willing and able to work with him to resolve his particular problems. But even if there were DOME Projects in every community, would there be scholarships available for every youngster who could benefit from such an opportunity? Of course not. Furthermore, it makes little sense to expect a handful of private institutions to do the job that is rightfully the responsibility of the public school system.

Carlos clearly believes that small classes, personal attention, and an environment in which he was encouraged to excel enabled him to make the transition from hooky player to successful college student. Voters across the country are saying they don't want to bear the tax burden necessary to make such functional school settings available to students like Carlos. They seemingly prefer to let their public schools become dumping grounds and use their money to send their own children to private school.

Neglecting our public schools will turn out to be a very poor long-range economic decision. How can we measure the value to society of the influence and leadership provided by youngsters like Carlos? As a bumper sticker I saw recently puts it: IF YOU THINK EDUCATION IS EXPENSIVE, WAIT 'TIL YOU'VE TRIED IGNORANCE.

Carlos would have been unlikely to become a dangerous felon, although who can confidently predict how any person will react to intense and protracted frustration? More likely he would have ended up on the street corner, drinking beer and measuring out his life in domino games and worthless policy slips just as many of his childhood friends are now doing. The waste represented by each of these unproductive lives is enormous. Yet we go on sanctioning this wasteful process and will continue to foster it so long as we value the potential of these young people less than that of children whose parents can pay for private alternatives.

Carlos has "made it," but the moral of his story lies not in his great good fortune or personal merit but in the tragic story of all the youngsters of similar merit who will never have the opportunity to rise above the failure and dependency our society expects from them. The public schools must make it their business, as perhaps they never have, to ensure that every child learns. So long as we go on neglecting the education of these forgotten youngsters, we will continue to create an angry and potentially destructive underclass of disenfranchised adults.

The educational system is not entirely to blame, however, for it only carries out the mandate it receives from the people who vote its budget and appoint its officials. We are the ones who must decide whether equal rights, job opportunities, access to decent housing, and quality education are fundamental prerequisites for a free and egalitarian society or only privileges for those fortunate enough to afford them. Unless we are willing to commit our energy and resources to making these necessities available to all who are willing to work for them, Carlos will remain a fortuitous exception to the tragic rule.

Chapter Eleven

Calvin: Disabled or Merely Stereotyped?

"I wish I knew how to talk to [my son] Benjie. I feel shy or ashamed when I want to speak my real feelings. Be fine to tell him that something nice can happen for *him* in life, something like how it is with me and Butler. One day I almost said it . . . 'Benjie, the greatest thing in the world is to love someone and they love you too.' But when I opened my mouth, I said, 'Benjie, brush the crumbs off your jacket.'"

ALICE CHILDRESS
A Hero Ain't Nothin' But a Sandwich

MACK: I had gotten to the point where I felt like hittin' my son, Calvin, all the time, and I don't believe in hittin' my children, so I knew I needed help.

Seems no matter what school I put Calvin in, something would go wrong. He wasn't learnin' nothin', and he was constantly in trouble. I went everywhere I could think of for help, but nothing changed. The people in the school system that have the most say-so, seems they couldn't do nothin' for me.

My daughter, Retha, kept tellin' me about The DOME Project and what it had done for her. Sure, it helped her pull her grades up, but it was more than that. Sometimes on a Saturday I'd hear her say, "I wish it was Monday." There was something there she really loved.

145

I thought there might be something like that for Calvin too. Lord knows, he needed it. I had decided there was no way he was goin' back to the school he had been attending. The place was killin' us both. If The DOME couldn't take him in, I was goin' to have to find some kind of way to send him out of the city.

Mack, Calvin's father, is a giant of a man who stands nearly six feet four and weighs well over two hundred pounds. He earns a living moving pianos, and I have often imagined he could pick one up and carry it by himself. Calvin, a wiry youngster with thick rimless glasses that gave him a quizzical appearance, seemed terrified of his father the first day they visited our program. I guess I would have been terrified also if I thought Mack might have considered hitting me.

Mack told me that Calvin was in a special education program for youngsters with minimal retardation or slight brain damage. I knew it would take nearly a year to get him reevaluated and returned to the main school population so he could be transferred to our program. Obviously Mack couldn't wait that long. When I asked Calvin if he wanted to try our class he mumbled so inaudibly that his father snapped, "Speak up!" Calvin winced and said again, in a hesitant whisper, "Yes, sir." Without further inducement, I decided to take him into the class immediately and deal with the bureaucratic consequences later. Mack had already decided to keep Calvin out of school if we wouldn't take him, so he wasn't worried about Calvin appearing on school records as truant while we tried to get him retested and approved for a transfer. We agreed that his legal status was less important than his physical and emotional well-being and trying to help keep his family intact.

CALVIN: At that time, everything was going berserk at home. Nobody was getting along. My father had hurt his back and was on disability. He was home all day with nothing to do, and I guess that made him grouchy. I was having problems with my stepmother too. She has a son that's younger than me. He would always be starting something with me, but if I hit him back I always got put on punishment.

Calvin was upset at the prospect of entering a new school. He had already attended eight different ones, mostly in rough neighborhoods, and each time he had moved he had to fight to show his schoolmates that he wouldn't let himself be bullied. During his elementary school years he had lived a somewhat nomadic existence with his mother and sister in various parts of the Bronx. His mother was very ill, and they never had much money, but Calvin remembers that part of his childhood as relatively pleasant and uncomplicated.

CALVIN: My reading was never very good, but I still liked school all right. I was pretty happy. I certainly never thought there was anything wrong with me or that I was different from other kids. I just used to daydream a lot. After my mother died, that's when I started to feel I had some serious problems.

After Calvin's mother died, Calvin and his sister went to live with their father in Manhattan. One of the first things Mack did was take them for a complete physical checkup. The doctors discovered that Calvin had a severe eye problem requiring surgery. While he was in the hospital for the operation, a social worker arranged to have Calvin evaluated for placement in the public schools' special education program. Mack knew Calvin had a reading problem and hoped the special education program would provide the extra help he needed. Instead it seemed to create a host of new problems that eventually led to Mack's threat to withdraw Calvin from school altogether.

MACK: I gave Calvin's teacher my home phone number, as I always do, and told him to call me if there was any problem. About two months later I went to pick my son up from school one day, and I noticed he's got this white patch over his eye. Seems some boy kicked him in the eye, and the school just put a bandage on it. I went inside to find out why the teacher didn't call me, and he says he didn't have my number. That didn't make no sense. Then, instead of tellin' me what happened, he starts to tell me there's something wrong with Calvin's brain. That really offended me. If he thought there was something wrong with my son, why did he wait until I went lookin' for him about something different to tell me about it?

I pulled Calvin out of that school and put him in another. This school turned out to be a really rough place, and just about everything that could go wrong there did. Calvin was always gettin' into fights. I told him that on account of his bein' little, people was always goin' to pick on him unless he learned to defend himself. He tried fightin' back, but it seems nothin' he tried did any good. After a while, he started looking for excuses not to go to school. If his head didn't ache then his stomach was hurtin'. Finally he dropped the excuses and just refused outright to go any more.

The Office of Special Education agreed to transfer him to a different school five blocks from where we lived. The problem was they insisted he had to ride to school in a special bus, and Calvin hated that bus. He could walk to school in under ten minutes, but because of the route the bus took he'd have to be ready for it more than an hour earlier. Then the bus would still get him to school late more than half the time. We tried all kinds of ways to get them to let him walk, but they wouldn't do it. I guess they just had to have a certain number of kids on the bus whether they needed to ride or not.

I gave Calvin's new teacher my phone number too, but this time I got the opposite reaction. Every least little thing that would happen, she'd be on the phone callin' me about it. I don't just mean once in a while. It became an everyday thing.

One day I went to her class to see how Calvin was doin' and found him sitting behind a partition that was separatin' him from the rest of the class. She told me he was there because he was cold. When I asked him he said he didn't have a clean undershirt that morning so he came to school without enough clothes. That didn't make no sense to me, but I went along with him and promised the teacher it wouldn't happen again.

A few days later I dropped by the classroom again. There was Calvin in the same place, behind the partition. This time the teacher said it was because he was easily distracted. I felt Calvin had a right to be a part of the class, not be separated off like that. I told her if she couldn't handle him I'd just keep him home.

I called the Office of Special Education every day for two straight weeks but couldn't find anyone willing to help me. Then someone finally said he'd look into the problem and get back to me, but I never heard from him again.

It wasn't just all the problems I was havin' with Calvin's schools, it was Calvin himself. He wasn't learnin' anything. I never saw him with a book, and he never had homework. Seemed to me like his teachers didn't expect nothing from him except to stay quiet and out of the way.

Teacher expectation frequently correlates directly with pupil performance. In one famous study, researchers informed some teachers that certain students' test results indicated they were entering a period in their lives during which they would be capable of exceptional improvement in their academic performance. Although the information was completely spurious and the youngsters had been selected randomly for the experiment, the "predictions" proved consistently accurate as the specially designated students scored significantly higher in their work while the control group's grades remained unchanged.

Negative expectations can be even more powerful. Teachers who don't believe their students are capable of excellence will not bring out the best in them. What is worse, low teacher expectations can be transferred to students, robbing them of self-confidence and motivation. Students who internalize a teacher's low appraisal of their ability or potential are unlikely to challenge those limits, much less rise above them.

This problem can be aggravated by racism and feelings of cultural superiority, whether conscious or subconscious, among teachers. By harboring doubts about the potential of students who differ from them in color or cultural heritage, they deprive those youngsters of an equal chance to learn and advance. This is as serious a violation of their civil rights as denying them a job later on in life, for the end results are likely to be the same.

Our West Side neighborhood is extraordinarily diverse, both racially and culturally. Whites trace their ancestry to every European nation. The nonwhite population is equally varied. In addition to substantial black and Puerto Rican communities, there are important concentrations of Dominicans, Haitians, Central and South Americans, and Asians.

Although the West Side is home to many different kinds of people, I would not call it integrated. While it is difficult to walk more than a few blocks without crossing into a neighborhood dominated by a different group, and a local shopping trip brings the shopper into contact with different kinds of neighbors and shopkeepers, there is little social interaction among members of different racial or ethnic groups.

The homes of most of the blacks and Hispanics, as well as many poor whites, are arrayed in a tunnel of poverty that runs along Amsterdam Avenue from Hell's Kitchen on the south to Harlem on the north. Rat-infested tenements and decaying brownstones line side streets that stretch like ribs on either side of the avenue, although a burgeoning brownstone revival movement is transforming increasing numbers of these side streets into enclaves of elegance. Once those crosstown streets hit Columbus Avenue on the east and Broadway on the west, however, white faces and elegant dwellings become the rule rather than the exception, culminating in the opulence of Central Park West, West End Avenue, and Riverside Drive. Thus rich and poor, white and nonwhite, live separate and very different lives within sight and sound of each other.

If integration is to work anywhere, it is likely to happen in a community where housing segregation patterns are not severe enough to necessitate busing children to achieve some semblance of racial balance. In our community, youngsters from varying racial, ethnic, and economic backgrounds can all walk to the same local schools. As one might expect, many wealthy families weaken this democratizing process by sending their children to private schools, but many middle-class families live on the West Side precisely because they want this kind of integrated experience for themselves and their children.

The four elementary schools serving the neighborhoods nearest The DOME Project attract an unusually heterogeneous student population. Enrollment figures from these schools indicate a pupil population that is 45 percent Hispanic, 28 percent black, 24 percent white, and 3 percent Asian. Somewhat surprisingly, these figures remain fairly constant through Intermediate School 44, the school to which these elementary schools send their graduates and from which we draw our students.

The most demanding classes at I.S. 44 produce well-prepared students. The I.S. 44 math team, for example, was for many years a dominant force in citywide competition. One year the A team finished first among eighth-grade entrants, and the B team was runner-up. Prevented by competition rules from entering a third team at the same level, the school jumped its C team to the ninth-grade competition, and it finished second. Nor should anyone assume that all of the school's top scholars come from the white quarter of the school's population. Black, Hispanic, and Asian youngsters regularly win their share of the prizes and commendations handed out for excellence and achievement.

It is at the other end of the scale of academic performance that racism persistently does the most damage. For although nonwhites share in the academic achievements of the school, the severe nonachievers are almost exclusively black or Hispanic. My first full year at I.S. 44, Luther Seabrook, the principal, ordered a reading test to be administered to all 1200 students during the first week of school to verify their ability to do the required work. Over 300 youngsters scored four or more years below their grade level in reading skill, indicating they were functionally illiterate and unable to do work appropriate for their grade. Among these nonachievers, only one was white.

Followers of Arthur Jensen and William Shockley might derive from those statistics confirmation of their belief that whites, as a group, will outperform blacks and Hispanics in intellectual endeavors because they draw on a superior gene pool. To Luther and me such unbalanced numbers indicated something particularly sinister about the way the public school system was failing to educate its students. Elementary schools are charged with teaching youngsters to read. That they should fail so miserably with 25 percent of them is a damning statistic in its own right, but that these figures should be racially determined is a scandal and a disgrace.

Asking youngsters who cannot read to achieve in school is as perverse as binding their arms and legs, throwing them into the sea, and ordering them to swim. Reading is central to a student's ability to function and affects his or her performance in every class. It is little wonder, therefore, that by the time a nonreader enters junior high school, the years of failure and frustration are likely to have inflated what began as a reading problem into a full-scale emotional and behavioral problem.

Some youngsters who cannot read become angry and rebellious. Others, convinced there must be something wrong within themselves, become complex-ridden and accustomed to failure. In either case, the youngster's ability to function in a regular classroom is severely impaired. Teachers who might be able to deal with such a youngster in a one-on-one relationship find themselves unable to cope with the same child in a class of thirty-five. Frustrated by the youngster's disruptive or reactive behavior, despairing of helping both the child and the rest of the class in the limited time available, the teacher may recommend placement in a special education program for emotionally handicapped children.

I recognize the need for school systems to provide special help for children with emotional problems. There is something deeply disturbing, however, about a situation in which the school system helps create emotional problems in certain youngsters by failing to educate them properly, then labels these same youngsters handicapped. When one looks at the racial composition of these special classes, the implications of what we are subjecting these youngsters to are even uglier. Blacks are overrepresented (20.3 per thousand) by a ratio of more than two to one when compared with whites (9.5 per thousand). Since 84 percent of the teachers making referrals for screening and possible placement are white, the likelihood that racism is a determinant in the selection process seems great.

From the first day Calvin entered our class, it was abundantly clear that he had problems. What we couldn't discern at first was whether he had sufficient resources to compensate for his weaknesses. He was very nervous and unsure of himself. He could barely read or compute. He spoke in a kind of protective mumble. When asked to read, even in a quiet corner with a single helper, he became downright inaudible. If assigned to write something, Calvin would spend ten minutes sharpening his pencil, arranging his paper, carefully copying his name and the date, then erasing and writing them over again. When he couldn't prolong this elaborate preparation any longer, he would find some other evasive tactic to avoid dealing with the actual assignment.

Calvin was not, however, a subdued or introverted person. We noticed that after the school day ended Calvin would suddenly become lively and expansive. He joined willingly in games and pranks with the other youngsters. We could even get him to do a little reading or math as long as we waited until the after-school program had begun. Apparently just the idea of being in school had become so oppressive to him that it curtailed his spontaneity and undermined his self-confidence.

Calvin obviously had real and resistant difficulty with numbers and the written word. His father told us he had a learning disability, but I had heard that so often about other youngsters that I paid little attention. Learning disabilities seemed to sprout everywhere during the seventies. An assistant principal at my son's public elementary school once told me 35 percent to 45 percent of his students suffered from them. Learning disabilities certainly can provide a convenient excuse for teachers looking to avoid full responsibility for their students' failure, but I am convinced they are really not all that common.

What we all have are different learning strengths and weaknesses. We have different learning styles too, and some don't mesh well with the teaching styles to which we are exposed. I learn languages easier than many people but have always had trouble with math. Some youngsters find phonics the simplest approach to reading, while others must learn to read with different techniques.

Several of my students have reversed letters and sounds in words while trying to read, but I have never worked with a youngster who consistently ran from home plate to third base instead of first while playing baseball. Most youngsters who reversed sounds and letters eventually learned to read satisfactorily. In other words, they had learning problems or weaknesses but not disabilities, since with adequate time and assistance they could compensate for whatever difficulties they were having.

We had to free Calvin from the fears and inhibitions holding him back. We used a lot of the same kind of tender loving care we had lavished on Ramon to convince him of his own personal worth. Calvin did most of his reading with someone's arm around his shoulder, and he could always find someone to sit and help him when he wanted to try writing something.

Slowly Calvin began to relax with us. We were, after all, the same people during school hours that he enjoyed horsing around with after three o'clock.

CALVIN: After so many years of not getting anything out of school, I had begun to feel the problem must be inside of me. That used to bother me a lot. But everybody at The DOME showed me my problems were really on the outside. Once I realized that, I knew I could get rid of them.

Teachers at The DOME helped me in ways that were somehow easier for me to understand. They played with me too. I stayed after school almost every day because someone always stayed to work with me. I never did that before. I could see that I was catching up, and that made me try harder. I didn't even daydream as much because I was having too much fun.

By the start of Calvin's second year in the program, his whole demeanor had changed. He had learned to speak out and look his interlocutor in the eye. He handed in his homework on time and even reached the point where he would take a regular turn reading aloud to the class.

Mack became one of our staunchest supporters. If his frequent conflicts with school authorities had made him seem difficult to get along with, perhaps that was because he wanted a decent education for his son and wasn't going to sit idly by, watching Calvin being reduced to an incompetent mumbler. He didn't have the kind of money that creates alternatives, so he had to keep hounding the public school system until he could get some kind of satisfaction.

MACK: I've seen so many changes in Calvin. Before, I couldn't get him to turn off the TV, but now I notice he'll sometimes stay in his room and read. He's even talkin' about college. That makes me feel good 'cause I know he really means to try his best.

Another thing, Calvin's not afraid of me anymore. I never wanted him to be in the first place, but I used to get so upset I'd come close to losing control. Big as I am, I guess it isn't surprisin' he'd be scared.

I think the way the adults at The DOME Project treated

him helped him a lot. They'd play with him, so he'd come home and want to do the same thing with me. At one time he didn't seem to know how to take me, but now we get along wonderful.

Calvin has been decertified from special education and is no longer burdened by an inappropriate label. He will never be a scholar and may not fulfill his dream of going to college, but he isn't mumbling to himself any longer or daydreaming his life away.

Calvin was lucky. He was only thirteen when Mack pulled him out of the destructive situation in which he was trapped. It is so much easier to help youngsters at that age than to rehabilitate them ten years later or support them through unproductive lives. Unless we can recognize the untapped potential in every youngster, regardless of race or learning style, we will continue to lose more Calvins than we reclaim.

Chapter Twelve

Tommy: When Survival Conflicts with Self-realization

"The bad nigger thing really had me going. I remember Johnny saying that the only thing in life a bad nigger was scared of was living too long. This meant that if you were going to be respected in Harlem, you had to be a bad nigger; and if you were going to be a bad nigger, you had to be ready to die. I wasn't ready to do any of that stuff. But I had to. I had to act crazy."

CLAUDE BROWN
Manchild in the Promised Land

I ONCE HEARD a father instruct his ten-year-old son: "If that kid ever bothers you again, Junior, break off a bottle and kill him!" The child looked absolutely horrified, as if all he wanted was to forget about the whole thing. On his own, the child probably would never have conceived of doing anything like that. Yet the father was a survivor, and who is to say he was not teaching a lesson that might some day determine whether his son would survive as well?

It is horrible to recognize the extent to which certain youngsters are forced to take stances for survival that are in flagrant conflict with their inner needs and drives. In the constant dialogue between nature and nurture, some youngsters are fortunate enough to be encouraged to grow and develop in ways consistent with their deepest feelings. Many, however, are not so lucky. Forced to confront a reality that demands constant responses inconsistent with their personalities, they risk permanent psychological damage.

Most youngsters live an extremely rich fantasy life. They all have feelings and fears they don't reveal to anyone. In certain neighborhoods, children learn early to communicate a sense of detachment, of being cool. At first a youngster may only adopt this attitude in appropriate circumstances, putting it on and off like a mask. Eventually, too much role-playing takes a toll, and the adopted behavior becomes a reflex, a part of the self. The inner person and the mask begin to fuse.

On my frequent visits to I.S. 44, I had often noticed a particularly handsome youngster preening himself in the reflection of a display case, chatting with girls in the hallway, or sparring with the older boys who hung out all day in front of the school waiting for their girlfriends. He wore a tiny earring in the shape of a crescent moon in the lobe of one ear and kept a cigarette perched behind the other. He reminded me of one of my first students, Julio, so vain about his appearance and reputation, so often high and walking a taut line between fear and bravado.

I learned the boy's name when an assistant principal called me in one day and pleaded with me to take Tommy into the class. I wasn't very enthusiastic, for I was having trouble getting those youngsters already in the class to settle down and do some work. Nevertheless, I agreed to meet with Tommy's mother.

Hannah grew up in southern Appalachia in a succession of orphanages and children's homes, and since the age of eleven she had been confined to a wheelchair. Once she was old enough to strike out on her own, however, she made her way to New York City. Not long after she arrived she met Tommy's father, got married, and had two children. The marriage didn't last, and Hannah found herself trying to raise her children in a welfare hotel called the Westbridge.

TOMMY: We moved to the Westbridge when I was eight months old and stayed there for seven years. The hotel never seemed like a strange place to me, but that must have been because it was the only place that had ever been my home. I used to spend my time riding my bike up and down the hallways or playing in front of the building.

One time, as I was leaving our apartment, the guy next door was stabbing another guy in his doorway. All I could see was this arm pumping up and down and blood squirting out of the guy like he was a fountain. I used to see people doing drugs in the stairway almost every day. But none of that was shocking to me. It was just what went on in the place I lived. It wasn't until later I realized all those things weren't a normal part of every child's life.

When the city finally agreed to resettle the welfare hotel families into decent accommodations, Hannah was offered an apartment in a city housing project on East 103rd Street in Spanish Harlem. At first she was very excited about having a real apartment of her own, but the move didn't work out well, and her excitement changed first to anxiety and then to unhappiness. Although her ex-husband was Puerto Rican, neither Hannah nor her children spoke a word of Spanish. She felt completely isolated in her new neighborhood, and Tommy and his sister had trouble making friends.

TOMMY: My mother used to tell us that people were beautiful, the whole world was beautiful, but in Spanish Harlem I ran up against a whole lot of mean people. Because of my mother and my light skin and green eyes, everybody started calling me "White Boy." I'm not ashamed of my mother or what I am, but I knew they meant that I was a punk who was afraid to defend myself. It was a rotten stereotype to be stuck with.

My reaction was, *I gotta show them I'm not a white boy.* I turned up my collar, put an earring in my ear, and tried to look as mean as I could. I had to fight all the time. I learned you can't take any shit, because once you give in even a little everybody's gonna step all over you.

HANNAH: I had mixed feelings when I saw what was happening to Tommy. I recognized that his behavior represented a way to survive, to avoid physical assault, and in that respect I saw it as a necessary thing. In another way I realized in order to do this Tommy had to curb a lot of what was good and human about himself, and I regretted that with all my heart.

TOMMY: I could never have admitted it to my friends, but I used to cry watching Bambi on TV. I had to learn to be bad.

I don't think I ever became a really hard person, but I couldn't just turn the bad-guy role on and off whenever I felt like it. Once I developed the image, I felt I had to live up to it. After a while, it began to influence my grades. Even if I felt like doing my work, I had to show everyone I didn't care.

Only at home could I relax and be myself. I could always be totally open with my mother. But as soon as I stepped out the door, I had to change.

After four years on the East Side, Tommy's family was able to transfer to a housing project back in our neighborhood. By this time Tommy had begun considering himself a tough guy. He hung out with older guys who were into drugs and fighting. He wasn't scared anymore, and he'd grown comfortable with the image once adopted only for protection.

Hannah probably should have begun cracking down on her son about this time, but she has never been a strong disciplinarian. Instead of imposing limits on Tommy's behavior, she tried to convince him to set his own.

HANNAH: I am really a very antiauthoritarian person. I guess it has a lot to do with being raised in an orphanage where everything was based on authority and nothing on love. Perhaps I'm still rebelling from that in some ways. I have a strong belief that children are not some kind of different species. I don't think I have the right to push my son around just because he's younger or smaller than me.

On the one hand, I feel people have to be responsible for themselves. Tommy has to come to terms with his own behavior. I don't think my imposing discipline on him teaches him how to do that. On the other hand, you pay a price for that kind of attitude. Your children sometimes indulge in horrible excesses and experience a lot of pain before they realize they have gone too far.

TOMMY: My mother never really pressured me. Maybe she should've. Ever since I was young, she would just try to reason with me. She never treated me like a child. If I did something wrong, instead of hitting me, she'd get upset and start crying. Sometimes I would've been happier if she'd smacked me.

I guess it had a lot to do with my father not being around. In some ways, I've always been the man of the house. I had a lot of responsibilities. Perhaps Mom used to slack up on me because she felt there was enough pressure on me already.

Single parents, once prevalent only in low-income neighborhoods, can now be found in large numbers in every stratum of American society. While their economic problems may vary, all are faced with the difficulties inherent in trying to raise children alone. Most of the single parents I know are women, and most work hard at jobs that pay relatively little. They return home to cook dinner, look after the children, and fall asleep in front of the television set. It is hardly surprising that such parents frequently show little enthusiasm for disciplining their children. The family has little enough time to spend together, for one thing, and there is a great need on the parent's part for that time to be pleasant. For another, imposing effective discipline takes patience and resolve, qualities an exhausted person is unlikely to possess at the times they are most needed. The presence of a second adult to lend support, listen to problems, and share the heartaches of child rearing helps reduce the temptation to follow the path of least resistance, doing what is easiest instead of what is best for the child. When a tired parent has to face alone the whole panoply of whining, pleading, threatening, and screaming, it takes more than desire and a theory of child development to persevere.

Poor single parents bear the added burden of their poverty. Not only must they contend with additional strain and hardship, but they often feel guilty about not being better providers for their children. One mother told me that she cries herself to sleep every Christmas Eve because she cannot buy her children the gifts they want. Even such necessities as proper dental care or shoes that fit correctly may be beyond the reach of the seamstress who arises at four in the morning, leaves breakfast for the children and resets the alarm clock, then takes the subway downtown for eight hours plus overtime at minimum wage in a claustrophobic sweatshop.

Welfare recipients, often characterized by the media as enjoying substantial benefits, have seen inflation cut the purchasing power of their grants down to crisis levels. The same week that New York City's Department of Consumer Affairs announced that the weekly cost of feeding a typical family of four had risen to over $100, a four-member welfare family could only get slightly under $50 per week's worth of food stamps. The total cash grant, excluding rent, provided just $1.27 per child per day for all expenses, a challenge for even the thriftiest shopper.

Poor people obviously cannot spoil their children by lavishing gifts on them, giving them too much spending money, or allowing them to have everything they desire. Instead, parents with little disposable cash are likely to indulge their children by allowing them to stay out late, eat junk food, watch too much TV, and avoid such unpleasant responsibilities as homework and household chores. Many youngsters in our program are consistently late for school. Upon investigation, we frequently find they don't go to bed on time. We try to correct this situation with the parent's help but often we discover that the adult usually falls asleep long before the child does and so cannot enforce a bedtime.

Adolescence is not a period when youngsters are likely to exhibit a great deal of self-discipline, yet it is a time when they must learn it to contend with the responsibilities that will come with adulthood. While many of the activities and routines youngsters are forced to endure in school are trivial and ultimately without value, so are many of the daily tasks and experiences of most adults. To the extent that school is supposed to prepare one for adult life, it probably does so best by helping students learn to tolerate frustration and crank out assignments. I have often asked my students to memorize Thomas Huxley's assessment that "perhaps the most valuable result of all education is the ability to make yourself do the thing you have to do, when it ought to be done, as it ought to be done, whether you like to do it or not." My soul rebels at this Calvinist reduction of education to petty discipline, but I realize DOME Project youngsters must learn it if they want to keep many important options open for themselves.

TOMMY: I have always been aware of the things I was doing wrong. The funny thing was that I kept on doing them. I just didn't have the ability to control myself.

In school, for example, I would cut classes for a few days. Then I would decide to turn over a new leaf. I would go to all my classes for a day, but I wouldn't understand any of what was going on because I had missed all the lessons leading up to what the teachers were talking about. Right away I would get discouraged. The next day, instead of trying a little harder, I'd forget all my good intentions, get stoned, and cut classes again.

Tommy showed up forty minutes late for his first class at The DOME Project. Everything about him — the way he looked and the way he sauntered into the classroom — announced, Here comes trouble! He handed me a report card that indicated he had been absent four days out of every five, and there was a string of zeros where grades should have been. Yet he had such an engaging manner that we all liked him immediately. In no time he made himself at home.

TOMMY: I didn't feel I had to prove myself to anybody at The DOME. There were only a few kids there, and some of them were already my friends. I said to myself, *Relax, there's nothing to worry about.* After a while I put my collar down and stopped carrying a knife. I began to see I really had a chance to pull myself up and made up my mind to try.

HANNAH: I think the most significant change for Tommy was that he saw the teachers had respect for him. From the first day he went to The DOME, people treated him as a person, not as a problem.

Our ability to treat each youngster as a person and not as a problem has undoubtedly played a major role in whatever success we have had, not only with Tommy but with Calvin and Carlos and all the other youngsters who have participated in our program. Many have come to us with terrible attitudes and behavior that was destructive to themselves as well as others. From the outset we have tried to make it clear to them that we cannot accept such negative attitudes and behavior patterns while taking pains to make the youngsters feel we are rejecting not them but their undesirable traits.

All these young people suffered from profound doubts about their own worth, making it difficult for them to criticize themselves or accept criticism from others. They had to believe we cared about and respected them before they could begin to profit from our advice. Unless they were prepared to listen to our comments and try to act upon them, all our well-intentioned admonitions were just so much wind.

These youngsters did not choose or create the particulars of their lives. Each of them had to cope with circumstances infinitely more complex and oppressive than anything I faced as a child or even knew about. My environment protected me from the very problems theirs inflicted upon them.

The pressures of modern urban living are toughest on those possessing the fewest resources with which to resist. Some of the young people described in this book absorbed more punishment from their environment than they could tolerate. Michael, for example, is in jail, serving time for aggravated assault. His anger and bitterness ultimately proved resistant to all the friendships he developed and positive influences he experienced with us. Isaac is still hanging out, waiting for the right situation to present itself, the golden opportunity that will magically transport him from rags to riches without requiring tedious or unpleasant efforts on his part. For these two friends, The DOME Project was an important refuge and support, but neither has yet found a way to parlay what he learned from us into the kind of life he would like to lead.

Some of our youngsters have fared better, but only after a protracted struggle to free themselves from a crippling sense of their own limitations. Ernesto now manages a small store in our neighborhood, and Ramon has just been promoted to a job in the data processing department at the investment bank where he has been working for several years. They both feel The DOME Project made the difference between their past failure and their present success. It is not unreasonable to suggest that they might still be floundering if we had not intervened when we did.

Our role in helping Carlos, Calvin, and Tommy seems almost too easy by comparison. Tommy works at The DOME Project helping junior high school truants deal with the problems that have been keeping them out of school, Calvin is a successful high school student, and Carlos is about to graduate and begin a career. All three of these young men responded eagerly and relatively rapidly to the opportunities we offered them. Their ability to help themselves once we pointed them in the right direction suggests these particular youngsters were not very different from those any of us might encounter in any other community.

And Lee? Lee disappeared for a while. His mother moved

away from our neighborhood, and no one saw or heard from Lee for over a year. Recently he called to say he was soon to be discharged from a residential alcohol- and drug-treatment center and would be looking for work repairing electrical appliances. He sounded good, but the test won't come until he leaves the facility and has to look after himself for a while.

Of the more than one hundred youngsters who have participated in our class since 1973, we have only lost track of two. Even those two will probably show up again some day. Many of the rest still live in the neighborhood. Some who seemed to gain little from the experience at the time stop by to visit and carry on as if their year or two with us was the most productive period of their young lives. As Ted said, maybe their relationships with us were the only decent ones they ever had.

Chapter Thirteen

The Additional Problems of Young Women

> *She does not know*
> *Her beauty,*
> *She thinks her brown body*
> *Has no glory.*
>
> *If she could dance*
> *Under palm trees*
> *And see her image in the river*
> *She would know.*
>
> *But there are no palm trees*
> *On the street,*
> *And the dishwater gives back no images.*
>
> WARING CUNEY
> *No Images*

UP TO THIS POINT I have written solely about disoriented young men, yet equal numbers of young women grow up in unhealthy environments amid horribly deforming circumstances. When I started The DOME Project in 1973, I balked at working with adolescent women, accepting only boys into the first class. By the third year a few girls began participating in the after-school and summer program, and our fourth class boasted a single resilient young lady and a dozen rowdy boys. Only recently have we fully integrated substantial numbers of young women into every program component.*

My initial reluctance to take girls into the program stemmed partly from a lack of confidence in my own ability to deal with young women's problems and partly from difficulties I experienced in recruiting appropriate female staff members. Feeling strongly about the importance of role models in influencing the behavior of young people, I thought I would be making a mistake trying to teach young women with an exclusively or overwhelmingly male staff. I subsequently realized that almost every young woman with whom we work has a strong, effective role model at home in the person of a survival-wise mother. The father is the one who is missing, and in many ways girls suffer as much from a father's absence as boys do.

Why the father is absent from so many of these homes is a well-documented but often misunderstood question. Dating back to the days when male slaves were sold away from their families and continuing to the time when an unemployed male in the household might jeopardize a family's eligibility for public assistance, black men have systematically been denied the role of provider in our society. The ability to provide adequately for one's family is essential to the self-respect of the head of any household. Many a father has left his home upon realizing his children would actually be better off financially if he were gone.

Earlier in this century this pattern changed temporarily as black and Hispanic men were enticed north to break strikes and keep wages low during a period of rampant industrial expansion. The sons and grandsons of these workers, however, are no longer wanted, as automation-minded employers now seek to reduce dependency on wage labor. Once again denied a productive role, these young men often resort to lives of crime and violence.

---

*The special problems facing the kinds of young women with whom we work deserve a much more thorough examination than I can provide. I offer the following insights and observations in the hope that others will follow with more detailed and profound commentary.

Young women also engage in criminal activity, but they are more likely to commit crimes such as prostitution, forgery, and shoplifting. Young men account for a vastly disproportionate share of the violent crimes and crimes against persons. While criminal activity is on the rise among young women, our society doesn't feel quite so threatened by female felons or the types of crimes they commit. Some version of Lee or Michael is more likely than one of their female counterparts to haunt our nightmares. Yet our curious ignorance of alienated young women and the experiences that help shape their lives costs us dearly in lost opportunities and wasted potential.

I first became aware that these young women are even more neglected than the young men who frequent The DOME Project when I tried to help Penny find a place to live. Penny is not a typical young woman by anyone's standards. She is a talented artist and dancer, extremely bright and articulate, and as mixed up as anyone I have ever known. She claims she was left in a basket on a church doorstep as an infant and raised in a foundling home, but Penny claims so many things that turn out to be either partly true or downright false that I never know how much to believe of what she says.

Penny came to work with us one summer as a participant in our work-training program. As we got to know her better, however, we realized Penny needed much more than a summer job. She needed an entire framework on which to reconstruct her life. Before she could begin she needed a place to live. Penny's only foster parents had died in an automobile accident when Penny was still quite young. Then began an odyssey of moving from institution to institution. I was horrified to learn when she started work with us that she was living in an addiction rehabilitation center despite having no drug dependency or drug-related problems.

The harder we worked to find Penny a place to live, the more it became evident how few options we were going to find for her. Had she committed a serious crime, there might have been halfway houses where she could stay and stipends for education or training. Had she been a heroin addict, a drug rehabilitation program would have been an appropriate placement. Had she been pregnant, she could have taken advantage of hostels, prenatal clinics, and counseling programs designed to meet a pregnant teenager's needs and those of the unborn child. But as plain unaddicted, unconvicted, and unpregnant Penny, she faced a world apparently unconcerned about her plight.

A protracted and discouraging search for adequate lodgings for Penny finally led us to a nun in the Bronx who had opened her home to young women with no place to stay. Once Penny was settled there, we succeeded in enrolling her in a college-level program for talented youngsters with the potential to do advanced work but who lacked a high school diploma. Penny eventually proved too undisciplined and irresponsible for both the school and Sister Ruth's no-nonsense hostel, but she at least saw some alternatives to the cycle of failure and despair that characterized her adolescence, if only she could develop the personal qualities needed to take advantage of them.

What upset me most about our difficulty in finding an appropriate place for Penny to live was the realization that available institutions seem to be designed to relieve society's fears or guilt, not to help the youngsters they ostensibly serve. Programs for violent or addicted teens separate potentially dangerous young people from the general populace but often don't offer much in the way of effective rehabilitation. Services for pregnant teens are apparently designed primarily to ensure the health and welfare of the unborn child (else why would there be so little concern for the same women when they are not pregnant?).

While young women have certain needs peculiar to the special circumstances surrounding their lives, they also share many of the drives and ambitions that motivate young men. In recent years women have been increasingly successful in breaking down the prejudices and stereotypes that have impeded their advancement, with many rising to positions of power and influence. Nevertheless, women must still generally outperform men to achieve comparable positions at every level. The young women who come to The DOME Project suffer from the same skills deficits and attitudinal problems that afflict the young men with whom we work. They would have a tough time holding their own in fair competition for jobs based on their limited competency even without the added handicaps of race and sex discrimination.

Young men who cannot compete in the marketplace may conclude that criminal activity offers the only realistic alternative to a totally passive and meaningless life. A young woman who cannot or will not compete has other options. She may attach herself to a dominant male, making a place for herself as his mate, or she may become pregnant and take on the role of mother. Although our society acknowledges the propriety of women developing other kinds of careers and lifestyles, plenty of pressure still exists for all girls to assume these traditional roles.

Adolescent women may be most prone to seek external support and solace when they attempt to break away from their mothers' control and assert their own identities. Those raised in single-parent families may also be looking for the fathers they never had. Increasingly these problems seem to cut across socioeconomic lines to afflict teenage girls of all backgrounds.

Myra was almost thirteen when her mother, Renee, brought her to The DOME Project. Renee is an imposing West Indian woman who had been raised by strict grandparents. She remembers having to kneel for hours on nutmeg graters in the tropical sun while holding a heavy book in each hand with arms outstretched as punishment for arguing with her grandmother. Now Myra, Renee's only child, was starting to argue with teachers and cut school, and Renee would not tolerate such behavior.

Myra made friends easily and enjoyed classes at The DOME Project. She frequently complained, however, of her mother's harsh treatment of her at home. She always had to be in by sundown, even when the midwinter sun set early in the afternoon. She felt her mother treated her like a baby except when there was housework to be done. Most of all, Myra resented her mother's refusal to let her accompany her friends to the discos and social clubs they frequented on weekends.

I basically agreed with Renee about the discos. They were not suitable places for thirteen-year-olds to socialize, nor was it safe to return from them unescorted late at night. Still, I could sympathize with Myra. There is nothing more humiliating than being treated like a child in front of peers who enjoy greater freedom and responsibility.

Shortly after the Christmas break, Myra ran away. For two days nobody could find out where or why she had gone, but gradually bits and pieces of the story began to emerge. On the third night Myra called her best friend to tell her she was staying with her boyfriend, Sly, in an abandoned building on the Lower East Side. Sly, a member of a gang notorious for its wild behavior, had apparently met Myra at a roller rink in the fall and had been seeing her whenever Myra could give her mother the slip.

The next two months were among the most frustrating I have spent at The DOME. Twice we managed to get Myra home, and each time she ran off again after a few days. Renee reported her disappearance to the police and filled out a petition in family court to have Myra picked up and placed under the court's supervision. We threatened Sly with prosecution for corrupting the morals of a minor, but he was only seventeen and knew he was unlikely to be convicted. He shrugged the whole problem off as being Myra's decision. We knew he certainly wasn't forcing her to stay.

Every second or third night, Myra would call me with a message for her mother. Several times she agreed to meet me to talk about how to resolve her situation, but most of those times she didn't show up. I spent many hours on desolate street corners late at night, waiting in vain for her to appear and cursing her lack of consideration.

Myra, meanwhile, was convinced she had found the love of her life. It didn't seem to matter that Sly sent her to work in a sleazy bargain store while he lay in bed listening to the radio and smoking pot. The more he demanded from her, the more important and needed she felt.

Sly finally ended Myra's romantic adventures by holding up at gunpoint the tiny grocery store on the block where he had lived all his life. Everyone in the neighborhood was outraged by his crime, and several people threatened to kill him if they caught him before the police did. The proceeds of the ill-conceived robbery were barely sufficient to pay for his escape, and he left Myra without a cent. He promised to send for her as soon as he could get some money together, but, predictably, she never heard from him again. Depressed, but with a new spirit of independence, Myra returned home.

MYRA: I thought I loved Sly at the time, but maybe I was just in love with the idea of being a woman. Sly made me feel important. I would've done anything he wanted me to.

I learned my lesson, though. Even before he pulled that crazy holdup, I began to see he didn't respect me.

I found myself thinking of Myra recently while sitting in the waiting room at the Men's House of Detention at the Riker's Island correctional facility. I had been waiting five hours for my sixty-minute visit with Michael and still had no idea how much longer I would have to wait. Perhaps 150 other visitors shared my discomfort. Some clutched a few cigarettes in their sweaty palms, but no food, drink, books, or newspapers had been allowed past the previous check-point.

My initial observation upon arriving at the reception center shortly after eight A.M. was that there were only a few white faces among those lining up patiently for visitor passes. In the waiting room I now realized I was doubly in the minority, for there were only three other men in the crowded hall: an elderly Puerto Rican wearing a brown felt hat, spinning a cane between his thumb and middle finger and occasionally flashing a toothless smile at the young woman sitting next to him; a tall, thin, silent, unsmiling black man with a wispy beard and long splayed shoes who slouched in a corner when he was not shuffling back and forth to the men's room; and a stocky Hispanic, fortyish, of dark aspect, who sat impassively, staring straight ahead, lighting one cigarette after another.

Except for a few toddlers alternately fidgeting in their chairs or scurrying across the dirty floor like crabs, all the rest were women. Many were just teenagers. Roughly one in four appeared to be pregnant. Some wore T-shirts announcing BABY or ANOTHER ONE ON THE WAY. Some simply bulged beneath light jackets pulled low to cover the open button at the top of their designer jeans. There were a few striking young women in the crowd, but all the women, even the pretty ones, seemed old before their time.

I mentally sorted those waiting so patiently into two groups. The larger group consisted of wives and girlfriends visiting their men. Myra would have been here, I realized, wearing her faithfulness like a badge. In these most frustrating conditions and depressing surroundings, the women were remarkably passive and unexpectedly good humored. Some casual teasing between a visitor and a guard sent ripples of laughter through the room.

Many of these women seemed to know each other. Perhaps they had seen each other on previous visits; more likely, they simply felt the comradeship engendered by shared hardships. Visiting their men in jail, for all the limitations of the situation, was still an important social occasion, and they managed it with all the flair they could muster. Their men, in jail or out, had become the focal point of their existence; visiting them was as much an act of self-affirmation as of affection or devotion. Were their roles reversed and these women locked away, I wondered, how many of the young men on the other side of the sliding steel slab would wait patiently week after week to visit their women?

There was another, smaller group of women in the waiting room, women grown shapeless and timeless through the mothering of generations, women invisible to all but those they had nurtured. I had waited with these women before in the emergency rooms of city hospitals, the interminable lines at welfare centers, and the airless anterooms of family court. Then I was constantly aware of their seething anger, their readiness to lash out in defense of their children. Now I sensed only resignation, a weight that hung from their shoulders like thick black shawls of sorrow.

*

If being the girlfriend of a "bad dude" engenders respect, a young woman can attract instant reverence by becoming pregnant. A girl ignored by everyone can win immediate recognition as a mother. A pregnant teenage girl can not only create a significant purpose to her life, she can do so without long and frustrating hours of remediation, study, or skills training. In too many cases the pain and rigor of child raising only impress themselves upon an adolescent mother's consciousness after the glamour of pregnancy and the novelty of caring for a newborn baby fade into the tedium of dirty bottoms, runny noses, late-night feedings, and the ultimate loss of freedom that responsibility for a dependent person entails.

When I was in high school in the 1950s everyone talked as much about sex as youngsters do today, yet I knew very few couples who actually had intercourse. But by 1972 a survey of unmarried women under nineteen indicated that 50 percent were sexually active, and by 1979 this number had jumped remarkably to 70 percent. Among the black teenage women interviewed in 1979, 88 percent had experienced intercourse. Ironically, the use of the Pill by teenagers has been declining dramatically in recent years, and 36 percent of those most recently surveyed reported relying on withdrawal, one of the least reliable methods of birth control.

A more permissive social climate is not the sole cause of

increased teenage sexual activity. A hundred years ago, when most young working-class women were seeking employment and starting to think about marriage at an earlier age than is typical now, the average age for the onset of menstruation was sixteen. Today the average age at which most American girls experience menarche is just 12.8, and 92 percent of all fourteen-year-olds have already menstruated. Meanwhile, the demand for blue-collar labor has declined and pressure increased to stay longer in school, greatly extending adolescence in both directions. Where a century ago a young woman might have been expected to menstruate at sixteen and marry by eighteen, she now is likely to begin menstruating by twelve but still be in school at twenty. These changes put a tremendous amount of pressure on young women to make decisions about themselves and their willingness to get involved in intense sexual activity — far more pressure than their grandmothers' generation experienced.

Sandra had her first menstrual period just before her tenth birthday. She remembers the excitement she shared with her fifth-grade girlfriends, waiting to see who would be the first.

SANDRA: We all used to talk about how great it would be. Having our period would make us women. But when mine came, I didn't think there was anything so great about it. It just made me feel miserable. I did notice, though, that the other girls began to treat me different, look up to me, so I thought maybe it would be worth it after all.

Physically a woman at ten, Sandra was pregnant by fourteen. She sincerely believed that once she began to mature physically her mother should treat her as having fully mature judgment. Sandra wanted to set her own hours and determine her own priorities. Her mother emphatically disagreed.

SANDRA: My mother wanted to control everything in my life. She told me I couldn't have a boyfriend until I was sixteen. I told her, "Ma, how are you gonna control the way I feel about someone. If you try to stop me from dating, I'll just find some way to do it without your permission." But my grandmother didn't allow my mother to date until she was sixteen, so she wasn't gonna let me do it either. I know she thought she was doing the right thing, but I thought she was being stupid.

Sandra was the most level-headed youngster in our class. She was frequently the mediator in disputes among her classmates, and they sought her advice on personal matters they would not share with the staff. But in her relationship with her mother, she was incredibly stubborn. She quickly discovered the limits of her mother's ability to impose effective sanctions and flaunted those limits whenever she chose. If her mother set a curfew, Sandra stayed out as late as she wanted; if her mother took away her key and threatened to lock her out if she returned too late, Sandra simply stayed out all night. Even the threat of being sent to a foster home didn't faze Sandra. She knew she was attending school regularly and hadn't committed any crime. She represented such a low-priority need for foster care there was virtually no chance of her mother getting her placed.

When Sandra got pregnant, she wasn't just playing ovarian roulette. She had decided to have a baby. She was very fond of the father but wasn't living with him at the time and didn't expect to marry him. Having a baby was not an expression of Sandra's conjugal devotion but a declaration of independence. She would give birth, find her own apartment, and leave the world of childhood and nagging mothers behind.

SANDRA: Having a baby gave me something to look forward to. A lot of people tried to get me to have an abortion, but there was no way I was gonna do that. I wanted to have the baby; that's why I got pregnant in the first place.

Sometimes a young woman will have a child because she can then apply for welfare benefits and her own apartment. Given the conditions under which many of these youngsters grow up, even the illusion of independence seems worth striving for. But it doesn't take long for reality to banish the dream. The adolescent mother is bogged down in the same struggle any other mother has to face, but lacks the perspective that emotional maturity can lend to the experience.

Some young mothers buckle under the pressure. Unwilling to sacrifice their social lives or independence, they either drop their children into the laps of more responsible relatives or give them up for adoption. Sandra, however, was intent on making a home for her son. She found a studio apartment in the Bronx and a job in a fast-food restaurant on Fordham Road. While a neighbor looked after little Hector for twenty-five dollars a week, Sandra spent eight hours every afternoon and evening slinging burgers and mixing malteds. Her apartment was broken into twice while she was out, and she lived in constant fear of the fires that ravaged her neighborhood.

Sandra continued to see her mother throughout this period. Although her mother never forgave Sandra for her behavior, she didn't carry the resentment over to her feelings about her grandson. She offered to let Sandra and her son move back into her apartment, but Sandra refused. Despite the hardships, she was in many ways happier living apart from her mother, and she was determined to make it on her own.

SANDRA: I'm just hard-headed, I guess. I don't really understand something until I've tried it for myself. I've never regretted having the baby, but I know life's gonna be harder for me. I don't want to work in McDonald's all my life, but I don't see how I can go back to school either. Even when Hector goes to school in a couple of years, I still got to pay the rent and buy groceries.

Two months after Hector was born, his father was stabbed to death in a sidewalk altercation over a drug sale. He had never shown much interest in his son, but his death brought home to Sandra how alone she really is. As a Hispanic teenager with an eighth-grade education and a child to support, she can hardly be considered to have rosy prospects. Yet Sandra is a survivor, and she shows every indication of being a loving and conscientious mother.

As much as she rebelled against her mother's efforts to limit her behavior, Sandra agrees that parents should help their daughters protect themselves from the perils related to their blossoming sexuality. The problem is particularly severe in families where both parents work or where a single parent tries to raise a family while working full time. An empty house or apartment provides an almost irresistible temptation to young men and women experiencing the normal adolescent urges for sexual exploration and fulfillment and the normal adolescent rebellion against parental authority.

While firm parental supervision probably curtails both temptation and opportunity for early sexual encounters, trying to isolate sexually maturing young women from their peers, as both Sandra's and Myra's mothers learned, is likely to be counterproductive. While fighting to give their children time to grow emotionally and intellectually, parents cannot merely repress their children's sexuality in an attempt to protect them. Sooner or later each child must step out on his or her own. A girl in particular will be infinitely happier when the time comes if she has gradually prepared for the kinds of problems she is likely to encounter.

*

Connie first came to us as a gangling, gap-toothed fourteen-year-old looking for tutoring help in math. By the time she turned seventeen she was a graceful and attractive young woman. The youngest of seven children, Connie adored her mother, a practical nurse who often worked long hours. Connie always had plenty of chores to do at home after finishing her homework at The DOME, but she never seemed to resent the responsibility.

The summer before Connie left for college, a dozen of the young women in our program asked me to take them on a week-long camping trip. I had taken a group of boys each summer for several years, and the girls complained they were being slighted. I had to admit they were right and agreed to rectify the situation. I figured I could take my son, Mikko, who was then five years old, along too. After numerous experiences with the boys, who had to be coerced into doing all the little chores necessary for survival in the woods, I was looking forward to an easy time with girls who were generally cooperative and used to looking after themselves.

We had to drive nearly seven hours to the campsite, and by the time we pitched our tents and ate supper it was bedtime. After making sure the girls were all ready to settle down for the night, I repaired to my tent, where Mikko was already sound asleep. I was almost asleep myself when a tiny voice outside the tent timidly called my name. I popped my head through the flap of the tent and stared straight into the unblinking eye of a flashlight.

"John, you'd better come," said Toni. "Something's wrong with Connie."

I hurriedly pulled my jeans and sweatshirt over my pajamas and stumbled over to Connie's tent. She sat sobbing quietly in the middle of the tent while two other girls tried to console her.

"What's the matter?" I asked.

"We don't know. She just keeps crying and crying."

At first I was frightened something might be seriously wrong, but Connie eventually calmed down enough to tell me she wasn't sick or in pain. She was frightened. I brought her and Toni back to my tent so the others could sleep and then tried to find out why she was so upset. She said she kept hearing noises in the woods, that she had never been camping before, and that everything seemed so strange to her. Only one of the girls had ever been camping before, however, and none of the others was having this kind of reaction. In fact, we had planned this trip because the girls had insisted on doing something different and adventuresome. Connie had been one of the instigators.

After a while, Toni drifted back to her tent while I struggled to stay awake in the hope of finding some way to calm Connie down and let her get some sleep. As a way of keeping the conversation going, I asked Connie about the last trip she had taken away from home.

"Oh," she answered, "I never slept away from my apartment before."

"You mean," I asked, dumbfounded, "you never slept over at a friend's house?"

"No, never," she replied. "A couple of times I slept over at my aunt's, but my mother always stayed with me. I guess I'm so scared because I'm used to sleeping with my mother."

Further probing revealed that Connie didn't only mean sleeping in the same house with her mother. She meant sleeping in the same bed. In her poor family there had never been enough beds to go around. As the baby in a family whose mother didn't have a husband or sleep-in boyfriend, Connie always slept with Mama. Now Connie was seventeen, ready for college, and she had never spent a night on her own. Of course she was scared of the woods. From what she told me, she would have been scared to spend the night alone in her own apartment.

Connie's situation was an exaggerated but by no means unique case. The culture shock many families experience when their Old World values conflict with permissive urban American norms and practices can trigger an urge to protect their children (especially their daughters) from what they consider an immoral society. As a result, many young women in the heart of New York City live an extraordinarily cloistered existence, which does, perhaps, protect them temporarily but also retards their transition to an independent adult existence.

While spirited and rebellious young women may experience too much, grow up too fast, and suffer tremendously as a consequence, those who are protected too assiduously from the realities of life may become unhealthily passive. Society already exerts tremendous pressure on young women to be passive and compliant. Youngsters who become submissive in a hostile environment where survival depends on resilience and assertiveness risk not only failure but annihilation.

It is possible to get a good education in many of New York City's public high schools, but students often have to fight in many ways to get what they want. They may have to push past drug dealers to get into the school building, ignore chaos and disruption in the school, and aggressively pursue the best courses and teachers. Students who sit back and wait are likely to get lost in the shuffle.

Many of the young women who come to The DOME Project for tutoring, dance classes, employment counseling, jobs, or any of the other after-school and summer activities we offer are considered good students by their teachers. From what I have seen of their skills and knowledge, I can only assume most teachers end up giving good grades to any youngster who attends regularly, hands in homework on time, doesn't disrupt class, and generally stays out of trouble. Apparently a pleasant demeanor, punctuality, and good handwriting have replaced intellectual accomplishment as the standards by which academic performance is measured. These girls may satisfy their teachers' desire for order and submissiveness, but their ignorance of the world around them is appalling.

One spring a senior honors student from a local high school asked my help in preparing for final exams in American history. She showed me a report card full of excellent grades, but she couldn't name the continents, tell me the difference between a governor and a mayor, or tell me how long ago Jesus Christ had been born. We had to spend hours learning to read a map and interpret a time line before we could even begin studying American history.

Another young woman proudly brought me a senior-year term paper on William Shakespeare for which her English teacher had awarded her a B+. She had not asked for help in preparing it, the student explained, because she wanted to see how well she could do by herself. The high grade apparently justified her confidence. One look at the paper, however, convinced me she had transcribed large chunks of reference material straight from library books and didn't have any idea what she had written. A brief discussion with her confirmed that she didn't know the meaning of many words in her own report, nor could she name a single Shakespearean play. In short, she had learned nothing from the experience except the mistaken notion that copying is an acceptable academic endeavor, and her teacher had let her come away feeling she had accomplished something praiseworthy.

Several young women in our after-school program have made it to their final year in high school only to discover they have too few credits or improper course distribution for graduation. Most had to spend an extra year in high school correcting a situation they could have avoided altogether had they pursued their own interests a little more aggressively and not left their education in the hands of teachers and counselors. These same young women are likely to accept jobs at less than the minimum wage or work overtime without compensation because they hesitate to demand their due. In its most offensive manifestation, their passivity keeps some of these young women from defending themselves or even protesting when they are sexually exploited or abused.

This kind of crippling passivity is not uncommon among women of all social classes. It contributes to such familiar situations as competent women stuck in menial jobs or acquiescing to subservient roles in social relationships. In the case of the poorest youngsters, however, it is also likely to lead to welfare dependency. Young women with minimal skills, accustomed to being told what to do, often find themselves unable to compete for a decreasing number of entry-level jobs and end up waiting for a monthly welfare check.

In a society as competitive as ours, it would be unusual for even this group to escape entirely the urge to compete. In young men, this drive to dominate takes many evident forms. They fight, play sports, and vie to see who can be most daring in the face of danger. Most young women shun these physical forms of competition, however, and deflect their competitive urge into striving for social status.

It is not difficult to determine which individuals in a group are the strongest, the swiftest, or the most agile. Direct competition produces a clear-cut hierarchy. In social matters, on the other hand, the only reliable measurement of status is the constantly shifting opinion of the relevant constituency. Those who would rise to the top of the pecking order must constantly curry the favor of those who will determine whether they will rise or fall. Thus adolescent women, a group already predictably unsure of themselves, often turn almost compulsively to others for encouragement and approval. Common as this insecurity is, its inhibiting influence on the emotional and intellectual development of young women can be significant. Our society has long encouraged women to center their lives around the approval and support of men. There is a great risk that adolescent girls will exaggerate this tendency, as Myra clearly did, when instead they should be exploring their own individuality.

Young women also get caught between their parents' desire for them to remain sexually quiescent for a few more years and the enormous cultural pressure to flaunt their sexuality. From Brooke Shields cavorting suggestively in designer jeans to a provocative Donna Summer crooning sultry disco ballads, the media constantly trade on sexuality, reaching out to impressionable youngsters long before they attain the age at which they can fully comprehend all the not-so-subtle innuendoes being bandied about. Youngsters are prodded into sexually precocious patterns of speech, dress, and behavior at an increasingly early age, and no one has yet analyzed the full implications of such a trend.

All these pressures can be terribly disorienting to a young

woman when she may be particularly ill equipped to handle them. Exceptionally skillful parents can help, but most parents find it difficult to deal with their own children's sexuality. Looking elsewhere for guidance, many adolescent girls find, like Penny, that either local teen programs pay insufficient attention to the special needs of young women or the only services available are designed to help girls who are already pregnant, have run away from home, or are otherwise in serious difficulty. We would be far better off were ample services available to young women in need of adequate counseling, confidential health care, career guidance, and activities that provide for a wide range of physical, emotional, and intellectual expression before they make irreversible choices. No one should have to become pregnant to acquire a feeling of self-worth or have a baby in order to create a useful social function for herself.

I have not mentioned teenage prostitution. Fortunately, although it exists on a massive scale in this city, I have had little direct contact with the problem. Nor have I touched on acquaintance rape, incest, and the various forms of child abuse inflicted upon boys and girls alike. I still have much to learn about the myriad deforming circumstances under which many young people are forced to live and try to grow.

Although I have already seen more than a lifetime's share of pain and suffering in youngsters with whom I have worked, there is too much to be done to allow myself the luxury of feeling sorry for either these young people or myself. I recently came across an eloquent passage in an extraordinary book, *The Road to Life,* by the Russian educator A. S. Makarenko. Writing about his experience as a teacher in the Ukraine in the 1920s, Makarenko's commentary reflects much that I feel about my own work sixty years later in New York City.

In the course of eight years I had been obliged to look upon not only the appalling woes of children who had been thrown into the ditch, but the appalling moral deformities of those children. I had no right to confine myself to sympathy and pity towards them. I had long since realized that to save them I was obliged to be relentlessly exacting, stern, and firm. I had to be as much a philosopher in regard to their sorrows as they were towards themselves.

This was my tragedy . . . It should be the tragedy of all of us, and we have no right to evade it.

PART FOUR

WHERE WE ARE NOW

Chapter Fourteen

The DOME Project: How It Grew and What It Has Become

There is no need to add to the criticism of our public schools. The critique is extensive and can hardly be improved on. The processes of learning and teaching, too, have been exhaustively studied. One thinks of the books of Paul Goodman, John Holt, Greene and Ryan, Nat Hentoff, James Herndon, Jonathan Kozol, Herbert Kohl; and of such researches as those of Bruner and Piaget; and of Joseph Featherstone's important *Report*. The question now is what to do.

GEORGE DENNISON
The Lives of Children

MORE THAN EIGHT YEARS have passed since I took five youngsters from I.S. 44 down to the basement of All Angels' Church and started the tiny alternative class that would grow into The DOME Project. Today there are four DOME Project classes with a total of sixty-five students from four different junior high schools, an outreach program attempting to help hundreds of chronic truants, an after-school program serving neighborhood youngsters from elementary school through college age, and a huge summer program that has become an important fixture in the life of our community. Our original budget of $5000 has swollen to nearly $350,000, providing for a full-time staff of seventeen, a part-time staff of twenty, ten VISTA Volunteer stipends, and all the supplies and services necessary to keep such a complex program operating smoothly.

The program grew not according to a plan or design but in a way I like to describe as organic. Each new program component was created in response to the perceived or articulated needs of young people in the community. Growing in this way has kept our energies focused on the most pressing problems facing our youngsters, but it has also kept us on the defensive, reacting to situations after they have reached crisis proportions. While we are gradually becoming better at anticipating these problems, lack of long-range planning remains a serious weakness of our program.

When I accepted Luther Seabrook's challenge in 1973 to work with a handful of students no one else wanted, I had no intention of creating a large program. I was merely working from day to day, trying to help those five particular boys. I had little experience on which to draw besides my own schooling and two and a half years at the Youth Center. Consequently my first efforts produced less a class than an anti-class, a loose association of five disaffected students and one ill-prepared and unlicensed teacher who all shared some notions of what we didn't want our class to be but had few useful ideas about how to structure an effective alternative. We created a clubhouse school, but as our problems multiplied I began to realize a clubhouse was not an appropriate model for the kind of learning environment these youngsters needed. I wanted a setting that was informal but serious. We succeeded in making it informal, all right, but the atmosphere we generated proved incompatible with the seriousness of purpose I was trying to establish.

By the time Ted came to my rescue in 1975, just before Lee attacked me with the utility knife, it was clear to everyone connected with the program that we needed to set firmer limits on the kinds of behavior we would tolerate. The program was also becoming too big to depend only on my limited energies and the support of a rapidly changing cast of volunteers and student helpers. We needed a more skilled and permanent staff, which meant I had to start raising more money.

The director of a small foundation, who had heard about The DOME Project through a mutual friend, began advising me on ways to strengthen the program. He suggested I pursue a variety of funding sources in an effort to diversify support for our work. A little informal research into how other programs supported themselves led me to the New York City Youth Board, the agency responsible for funding youth development and delinquency prevention programs in New York City. For several months the proposal I submitted to them apparently went unnoticed. Then suddenly, inexplicably, two Youth Board officials summoned me to a meeting in the spring of 1978 and explained that a substantial matching grant was being rushed through for us. We would be able to draw down a certain amount of public money if we could match it with private contributions. They spoke enthusiastically about our program and assured me that support, once given, would be available annually as long as we met the terms of the contract.

I was too excited about the prospect of getting a renewable contract from a municipal agency to ask why the Youth Board had at first ignored my request and then approved it so hastily. Later I discovered, to the embarrassment of everyone concerned, that the officials who had contacted me thought they were dealing with the director of the Door, a much larger and better established program. By the time the Youth Board officials realized their error, they had gone too far to back out gracefully. Thus one of our most significant advances, enabling us to hire desperately needed staff and attract additional grants, resulted from a simple mix-up between very different programs with confusingly similar names.

I used the Youth Board money to hire Scott, Omar, and George. Scott, raised in the housing projects behind Lincoln

Center from which The DOME Project draws many of its students, had been an active teenage participant in Youth Center activities when I worked there. A recent college graduate, he had become interested in working with youngsters. Omar, another former Youth Center participant, had moved to our neighborhood from the Dominican Republic as a young man. He left community college to play professional baseball, but his career was cut short by injuries. George grew up in the Bronx, went from public school to Columbia University, and at the time I hired him was studying for a master's degree in education at Bank Street College. As a student teacher at I.S. 44, George had become interested in our program and volunteered many hours at The DOME.

Youth Board funding transformed The DOME Project from a marginal program with a precarious month-to-month existence into a small but relatively stable community organization. We acquired a racially and ethnically diverse staff, all of whom had had previous experience with our project. The Robert F. Kennedy Memorial helped us meet the matching stipulations of our grant, and for the first time we had a budget that began to reflect the importance of the work we were trying to accomplish.

George now coordinates all classroom activities, teaches science, runs our photography program, tutors, and helps coach the girls' softball team. Scott teaches math, tutors, runs a silk-screen printing program, and helps out with the basketball leagues. Omar teaches social studies, coaches baseball and basketball teams, and directs the recreation component of our summer program. I teach English, tutor a little, coach the girls' basketball team, and have overall administrative responsibility for the program. Technically I am the only teacher for the class, the only person licensed to provide instruction. In reality, I am usually the least well-prepared and least effective teacher of the four. George, Scott, and Omar, who are paid as counselors and after-school aides, have become skilled instructors who carry most of the burden for our classroom program. Someday I hope to have the opportunity to discover how well I can teach, given adequate time and energy to prepare lessons, but for now I recognize that my administrative duties severely limit the attention I can pay to my teaching chores.

A typical day for us begins, as it has since 1973, at 8:00 A.M., when I clock in at I.S. 44 and pick up the school breakfast. By 8:20 I am at The DOME, and students and staff begin arriving shortly thereafter. At nine o'clock, George, Omar, Scott, and I station ourselves in the two rooms where we hold classes. Our twenty students split up for individual or small-group instruction, choosing the subjects they prefer or need the most help with at the moment. Although youngsters can choose when to take each subject, they must participate in a certain number of classes and complete a certain number of class and homework assignments in each of the four disciplines every week.

We have found that our youngsters don't react well to frequent interruptions, so we hold fewer but longer classes than most schools. We begin with a more or less flexible eighty-minute instructional period followed by a short meeting in which we discuss trips, problems, and other class business. Then the youngsters get a ten-minute break when they can go outside, get a snack, or just fool around. Another eighty-minute period leads up to lunch. After lunch comes a long class period we may use for special projects, regular classes, trips, gym, or swimming at a municipal pool.

All of us have different teaching styles. Scott likes to challenge his students. Sometimes his class seems on the verge of breaking into a small riot, but the students enjoy the competitiveness and Scott's active style. Omar's classes are more reflective. He is very interested in language and the students' ability to understand and communicate complex ideas. He became so distressed at his own shortcomings that he enrolled full time in night courses at City College and has nearly completed studies for his degree. His enthusiasm for studying bubbles over into his own classroom work, and his persistence serves as an excellent example for our students. George is a restless perfectionist, always searching for a better way to present ideas and involve youngsters in the learning process. He is very creative and helpful to the rest of us in suggesting teaching methods or aids that might make our work easier or more effective.

While we work with our class of twenty in the manner just described, three other classes patterned loosely after ours are held in other parts of the school district. How they started makes another interesting story of the way our program sometimes backs into progress. Because I finally got my teaching license at a time when municipal budget cuts were provoking massive layoffs of tenured teachers, I had to raise funds for my own salary for two years while the Board of Education held up all new appointments. Then, when I finally won a job, the school system kept laying me off or reassigning me every summer, forcing me to fight tooth and nail to recapture my job each September.

I never felt secure in fighting openly for my job because our program had not been properly sanctioned by the local school board. About the time my second child, Elina Miriam, was born in 1977, I decided to challenge the school board to legitimize our program. To my surprise, they not only endorsed The DOME Project class but asked me to help set up replica programs to serve each of the three other junior high schools in the district. The principals recommended teachers they thought would do well with difficult youngsters in off-site settings, and by the opening of the 1979–80 school year we had three new programs in place.

Each of these classes has its own personality. Project Youth Expression, housed in a converted Harlem school building, combines an intensive basic-skills program with an exploration of the history and culture of Harlem designed to enhance the students' self-awareness and self-esteem. DOME 54, located in a community center in a predominantly Hispanic section of our community, is a bilingual and bicultural program offering intensive instruction in fundamentals within a setting that respects the strengths and assets of the students' native culture. Discovery Workshop, an open education project in a church basement, emphasizes individualized instruction and exploration of diverse learning experiences.

The licensed teacher in each class is supported by an unlicensed DOME Project instructor-advocate and as many interns, volunteers, and trainees as we can recruit. Nonsalaried workers fill many of the staffing needs of our program and constitute an extremely valuable community resource. Ever since Miriam helped me get through my first semester of teaching, I have appreciated the contribution such volunteers can make. I also realize a program must provide adequate support for volunteers to keep them happy. They may need supervision, materials, a clearly defined role, and encouragement when the going gets rough. Many wonderful volunteers have found their way to us only after unsuccessfully offering their assistance to public schools or social work agencies that either didn't know how to utilize them or weren't willing or able to alter routine procedures to make room for them.

In addition to volunteers from the community, we regularly agree to supervise and train high school interns and CETA (Comprehensive Employment and Training Act) enrollees. What these workers may lack in skills and sophistication they often make up for in enthusiasm and common sense. We have hired as full-time staff members several of these trainees and interns. Recently we have also begun to supervise college students seeking field study placements in counseling and education.

While these workers assist the teachers in our alternative classes, other staff members attend to many different kinds of important business. Our Juvenile Justice Advocate may be in Family Court with a youngster, sizing up a group home, or helping defuse a crisis in the streets. The Youth Employment Counselor may be writing a proposal, contacting a prospective employer, or preparing a training session for young people interested in finding jobs. A staff member who deals with the special needs of young women may be meeting with school officials about a sex-education program, escorting a student to a health clinic, or seeking child care for a teenage mother who wants to return to school.

In addition to these ongoing activities, we have recently undertaken a major drive to reduce truancy in our district. We have an Outreach Coordinator, a staff Outreach Worker, seven VISTA Volunteers, and one CETA trainee working full time trying to determine the major causes of truancy and create some effective responses. Troublemakers who disrupt school become the squeaky wheels who get all the attention, but truants are routinely ignored or even subtly encouraged to stay away from school by teachers burdened with overcrowded classrooms. Reduced school budgets have cut deeply into the number of attendance officers available to track down absent youngsters. Our district, with nearly 12,000 elementary and junior high school students in twenty-three different schools, has just three attendance teachers to monitor the 1500 to 2400 absentees each day. They can barely complete all the required paper shuffling, much less have an impact on the truancy rate.

Truancy, in the final analysis, is less a problem than a symptom. A youngster who stays away from school may be reacting to many difficulties. Problems at home, fear of failure, a dislike for school policies or personnel, personal anxieties — the list is virtually endless. Among the truants with whom we work, we find youngsters who are pregnant, youngsters who have serious drug problems, youngsters who are afraid of their schoolmates, and youngsters who simply hate being humiliated day after day. Adults working in situations where they are regularly held up to ridicule would be expected to quit. Youngsters who try to quit school before the permitted age are breaking the law.

Walking away from school may not be a very effective way for these youngsters to deal with their problems, but it is frequently the only solution they can find. We try to reach out to them and suggest an alternative or more appropriate course of action. Sometimes we end up acting as advocates on the student's behalf. At other times we are a resource for youngsters looking for help but unable to contact people who can provide it.

Our outreach staff members have discovered that many truant youngsters will return to an alternative school setting in which close personal relationships and more flexible policies prevail, but not to a traditional school setting. As a result, we have begun organizing a movement to create additional alternative programs in our district. We believe such programs can have a significant impact on truancy as well as providing appropriate schooling for many youngsters who attend regularly.

*

After school, The DOME becomes, if anything, even busier than during the school day. Some of our students leave, but others stay behind to participate in the many activities that begin once classes have ended. Chief among these is our tutorial program. Tutors include teachers from the various DOME classes, college students with work-study grants, high school students getting service-learning credit, and many volunteers from the community. Participants include elementary school youngsters struggling to learn to read and ambitious high school students trying to improve their chances for admission to competitive colleges. We work with youngsters with special problems as well as youngsters who merely want a congenial atmosphere in which to do their homework.

Originally we created the tutoring program to help the first graduates from our class cope with the demands of high school. Gradually, however, our other activities began to draw additional youngsters into the program. To our dismay, the appalling level of underachievement Arthur and I had noticed in the first youngsters we worked with at the Youth Center continues to plague a majority of the bright students who find their way to The DOME Project. They produce work far below their often considerable potential and seem generally unaware of how much they miss by doing only the barest minimum needed to pass their courses.

While the basis for our tutorial program is help with homework, we try to go beyond this essentially unrewarding level and find ways to help our youngsters develop good work habits, take pride in their work, and nurture what little intellectual curiosity the school system hasn't completely snuffed out. Given the extraordinarily low level of competence required to do acceptable work in most of their schools, we feel it is essential for them to acquire personal standards of performance appropriate to their own abilities if they are to acquire a functional education.

*

William, a student who came to The DOME to play basketball, impressed me from the start as particularly sensitive and alert. I could tell, however, that he didn't take either himself or his future prospects very seriously, so I began encouraging him to spend some time studying with us after school in an attempt to raise his sights. Although his ninth-grade report card indicated he had only a 66 percent average, that figure placed him in the top third of his class. He didn't read well and his writing was atrocious, but he was a bright youngster and a willing worker. The first semester he came to us for tutoring his average shot up to 88 percent, and in his junior year he followed Carlos to private school in New Hampshire. By 1980 he had entered college after working for a summer as a teller in a major commercial bank. I wish I could say William represented the rule instead of the exception, but his story does indicate how even a modest tutorial program can sometimes start a youngster on the path to personal growth and achievement.

*

While tutoring is central to our after-school program, we also try to provide a range of activities that address the varied developmental needs of our youngsters. For example, during the 1980–81 school year we ran three basketball leagues involving eighteen teams and placed three teams of our own in citywide competition. We set aside one evening a week for volleyball instruction, and some time is left open for free play. Jose, who works as an instructor-advocate in one of our satellite programs, coordinates recreation activities, and the rest of the staff help out by coaching teams or officiating games.

We try to keep our sports program's goals and objectives in balance with the concepts that underlie the rest of our activities. We emphasize participation by everyone who wants to play, leading to much initial grumbling by the more competent players but a better eventual appreciation of the appropriate role of competitive sports in the life of a community. Our program stresses good sportsmanship over winning, no easy task among youngsters deprived of other means of achieving excellence and accustomed to measuring their own self-worth through athletic achievement.

We recognize that physical activity is important for the healthy development of every child, but most youngsters find ways to get more than enough exercise. Our objective is to achieve a proper balance between sports and other activities that youngsters may find less enticing at first but that may ultimately prove more beneficial to them. Thus we expect our recreation program to draw youngsters into The DOME Project, but once we get them involved we encourage their participation in many kinds of activities that will sharpen their intellectual skills and broaden their social perspectives as well as strengthen their bodies.

Our cultural enrichment program is designed to put youngsters in touch with their feelings and expand their awareness of their history and culture. Activities include ballet and jazz dance classes, drama and mime, song writing, cultural history, photography, and silk-screen printing. Skilled youngsters and novices work together in ways that enhance cooperation and mutual respect. Most of the teachers are professional artists, but few of the young people are interested in pursuing artistic careers. They simply get caught up in the enjoyment of expressing themselves or learning a new skill.

Both the recreation and cultural enrichment programs help youngsters develop self-confidence and acquire self-discipline. These qualities, which many of our program participants initially lack, will later prove invaluable to them when they seek employment. We pay careful attention to the kinds of progress our youngsters are making toward employability because their ability to get and hold jobs will greatly affect the quality of their adult lives. This concern has led to our extensive involvement in employment training and pre-employment preparation.

Most of our youngsters have an imperfect understanding of the connection between academic performance and employment readiness. They see no similarity between completing an onerous homework assignment and completing an unpleasant task for an employer. Because one activity produces an immediate, tangible monetary reward and the other doesn't, many young people mistakenly assume they can take a cavalier attitude about schoolwork but will somehow instinctively know how to deal with work assignments when money is due. We try to get as many youngsters into work situations as early as circumstances and the law permit to show them, before they have to learn it the hard way, that responsibility is not a trait that is casually developed.

For young people in our program, part-time employment is important in many different ways. An after-school job can provide a crucial income supplement for hard-pressed families. Many of our youngsters spend their paychecks not on records and candy but on clothes and other necessities. When a welfare mother has only pennies a day for food and clothing for her children, and sneakers average $30 a pair, an after-school job may make the difference between the humiliation of coming to school in tatters (or playing hooky to avoid that humiliation) and taking pride in one's appearance. As Ramon pointed out, when the rent is overdue and there isn't enough food for the family, even a pencil for school can become a luxury.

Since 1973 we have run many kinds of part-time and full-time employment programs. Our experience suggests there is really no such thing as a single ideal program. Different youngsters have different needs, and we serve them best when we have a range of programs to offer, allowing us to match a youngster to the component that best suits his or her specific strengths and weaknesses.

Most of our youngsters need to start with an in-house program consisting of tasks within The DOME Project. They may work as recreation aides (coaching, keeping score), tutors, cultural program aides (assisting a dance or art teacher), or clerical assistants. These jobs, generally requiring minimal skills, allow them an initial work experience within a familiar and nonthreatening context. They work with people they know and from whom they are already accustomed to accepting advice and criticism. We teach them to be punctual and responsible, the consequences of lateness or absence, how to deal with misunderstandings, and the relationship between hours worked and pay received.

Some youngsters are remarkably naive about the nature of working relationships. Raised in families where no one works and the only source of income is a welfare check, which arrives every two weeks even if no one leaves the house, they must learn about employer expectations and the most fundamental assumptions every worker should have before accepting a job. For example, we always find a few young people who cannot understand why they have to wait until a pay period has ended before being paid. They don't expect withholding taxes to be deducted from their pay. Often youngsters will anticipate a week's salary and borrow against it before actually being paid. If they miss some time during that week, their pay checks will not reflect the sum expected. Unable to make the connection between the time actually spent on the job and the amount on the pay stubs, many youngsters angrily demand to know what we have done with their money.

Once youngsters can cope with these minimal responsibilities and conform to minimal employer expectations, we like to place them in other not-for-profit work settings such as hospitals, museums, day-care centers, public radio stations, or senior citizen centers. Here they must meet new people and respond to a new environment. Since there is no pressure in such settings to increase profits or beat out the competition, staff can generally take the time to train our youngsters or answer their questions. Moving out of our center is often a big step for program participants with limited self-confidence, and working in a different kind of nonprofit program that shares similar values with The DOME has proved a valuable transitional experience.

Once our youngsters have shown they can handle the demands of a different work place, they may be ready for private sector employment. We have worked hard to convince local employers that our program constitutes a valuable resource for them. We can usually locate temporary and part-time employees on a moment's notice and often provide them with specific training. When the owner of a small publishing house who had hired one of our young men realized the youngster couldn't handle routine shipping tasks because he had an insufficient grasp of geography, we hurriedly tutored him on everything from reading maps to finding zip codes. By supporting our youngsters in this way, we help them learn important skills, and employers appreciate not having to divert valuable staff time to additional training.

Sometimes employers recognize a young worker's potential and actively seek to train a youngster for further responsibilities. A local paint-store owner agreed to supervise a DOME Project youngster, Leon, who had a severe learning problem, as part of a subsidized training program. Although a teenager,

Leon could not read even the simplest books. He had begun hanging around drug dealers, trying to establish an identity for himself on the street to compensate for his lack of stature and success in school. However, once the job opportunity arose, he jumped at it as an alternative way to create a positive self-image. The store owner, a good-natured but shrewd businessman, was impressed by Leon's seriousness and willingness to learn. When the subsidized program ended, he offered Leon a part-time job in the store. Two years later Leon still works there. He has learned to take orders over the phone and fill them from written forms. He handles inventory and deliveries. He is still not a very successful student in school, but he has learned rapidly every skill required for advancement on the job.

An even more dramatic case involves Sammy, a young man who dropped out of junior high school in 1973 and attended classes at The DOME Project for almost two years as a daily drop-in. He had adequate skills to do well in class, but his home life was in such a shambles he simply couldn't tolerate a business-as-usual school day. I watched him become ever more seriously depressed as his mother and brother died, then as his father sank into an alcoholic paralysis. Sammy began speaking to me of suicide, but he wouldn't allow me to help beyond listening to his troubles. Sometimes he was so choked with sadness he couldn't even talk.

One day the head of a textile firm who knew of our program called and asked if I could recommend a youngster who would like a job delivering textile samples. I sent Sammy, who, within two months, completely reorganized the company's stockroom and learned the shipping and receiving end of the business. The company eventually sent Sammy to night school to learn more about fabric. He now runs his own small department with several assistants he has recruited and trained himself. He is married, has his own apartment, and I am convinced the job saved his sanity and perhaps his life. In return, the company got an exceptionally competent, diligent, and loyal worker.

Not all our work experiences are aimed directly at employment training. We design many of our projects as service-learning activities in which the participants make significant contributions to their community while acquiring new skills. Such projects teach young citizens a sense of responsibility to others.

Our most successful service-learning project to date has been the development of a luxuriant community garden on what had been a rubble-strewn lot. In the spring of 1977, we began cleaning up a dangerous and unsightly lot adjacent to a Loew's theater on West Eighty-fourth Street and Broadway. After a summer of grueling work, during which we cleaned the entire lot, brought in soil and fertilizer, and began planting shrubs and vegetables, the realty branch of the Loew's Corporation ordered us to leave. When we complied the property began to accumulate debris and animal feces again.

After picketing the theater to protest Loew's unneighborly behavior and force them to make some efforts to clean the lot, we shifted our attention to a city-owned lot one block away. Our youngsters were understandably upset about starting over. Cleaning the lot was the most onerous and least rewarding part of the job. They complained at first but gradually settled down to prepare the lot for planting. After removing all the garbage and collecting all the broken brick and mangled pipe, they began carrying railroad ties and soil from the Loew's site to our new lot. Although we only received permission in July to work on the lot, we were ready to harvest a crop of vegetables by September. The youngsters were particularly pleased with the enthusiastic reception they received from community residents. Working together helped break down many prejudices and stereotypes that summer and began to establish our program's reputation in the community.

Our neighbors were not alone in appreciating our efforts. We had borrowed tools from the Council on the Environment of New York City, a technical assistance program dedicated to improving the urban environment. When an anonymous benefactor offered financial support for self-help groups that were creating urban gardens in New York, the Council helped us secure a grant. We ordered topsoil, sod, shrubs, and trees. We landscaped the lot and installed a ten-foot-high iron fence. By the time we had worked on the lot a full year, our modest garden had become one of the most beautiful vest-pocket parks in New York City.

Working in the garden taught our youngsters some botany and soil chemistry. More important, perhaps, it taught us all to take greater pride in our community. Many other community residents told us how proud they were of the garden, and many volunteers helped us maintain and protect it. Since we began working on it, there have been no significant acts of vandalism. Everyone has had a hand in planting or watering or tending the trees, shrubs, flowers, and vegetables, so no one considers destroying them.

The garden forced us out of our basement center into the street and convinced us it was time to apply some of our enthusiasm to increasing the community's awareness of our presence. Instead of holding our 1979 summer program inside the church and limiting participation to youngsters already in the organization, we chose to move the entire operation to the schoolyards occupying the same block as our garden. Omar ran softball and basketball leagues in which every team was coached by a youngster from our program. For children of elementary school age, other youth participants ran a summer day camp that included trips and daily sports and craft activities. Some youngsters continued to work in the garden while others photographed the various activities we had organized. Shigemi ran a health project in which the young participants learned first aid, how to conduct health screenings, and how to hold exercise and nutrition classes for senior citizens.

All these activities created a very festive atmosphere on West Eighty-fourth Street, a block many people were previously afraid to walk on. We quietly but firmly moved the drug dealers off the block and away from the playgrounds. We kept the area clean and virtually eliminated all fighting there during the daylight and early evening hours, when the program was in operation. Hostile racial and ethnic groups that had used those play yards as a battleground now converged on them to cheer on their favorite softball teams or participate in a friendly game of volleyball.

As local residents became increasingly aware of our work, they began approaching us with problems not directly related to education or youth development. Many of our youngsters lived in decaying buildings. Unable to maintain these rent-controlled tenements, pay taxes on them, and still turn a profit, some landlords chose to milk the rent rolls, default on the taxes, and abandon the buildings. A dozen such buildings in our immediate neighborhood fell to the city's care, and the city hardly proved to be a better landlord than its predecessors. Tenants complained that the city was slow to make even emergency repairs and seemed incapable of maintaining essential services.

Before the city had held these buildings very long, real estate values in our community began to rise at an astounding rate. Suddenly developers and speculators were expressing an interest in these buildings. That interest, however, did not necessarily extend to the occupants, whose leases would stand between the investors and windfall profits.

Working closely with local officials, a neighborhood housing group, and a nearby settlement house, we at The DOME Project began organizing the tenants into formal associations. At the same time we helped form an ad hoc coalition of thirty community groups (churches, antipoverty agencies, day-care and senior citizens centers, parents associations from public schools, etc.) to support the tenants' right to stay in our community. We held a massive street festival in May 1980 to publicize our concerns and rally community backing for the steps we planned to take. Our first block party, now an annual event, drew over 5000 people, raised $3500 for the coalition, and convinced many of the tenants they had the support of people capable of effective action.

New York City has a number of admirable housing programs that allow tenants to develop their own alternative plans to city management. These programs allow for an interim period during which tenants can select a certified managing agent or demonstrate that they are capable of managing a building themselves. Then they are given the option of buying their own building and putting it back on the tax roll. Perhaps because of the skyrocketing real estate prices, which promised an unusually attractive return to the city if these buildings were sold at auction, city officials suddenly appeared to become reluctant to accept any buildings in our neighborhood into their alternative management programs. The tenants, coalition members, and elected officials kept up the pressure, however, and in 1981 the city finally relented.

Construction trainees from the settlement house's urban rehabilitation program began making repairs in several of the buildings. Tenants and community residents joined to clean up yards and alleys layered with years of debris. Many tenants who had withheld rent from the city to protest lack of services or other serious violations began paying it every month to their tenant association.

The limited but highly visible success our housing coalition achieved in this struggle has awakened a lively interest in civic affairs and a new sense of optimism in a portion of our community previously resigned to powerlessness and exploitation. I don't mean to suggest that The DOME Project should take credit for this change, but we played a significant part in stimulating it. What makes this phenomenon all the more interesting is the interconnection between our original role as a small alternative public schooling program and our expanding role as catalyst for community change. Our specific service functions establish our constituency and validate our right to speak out on matters of general concern to the community, while our activism helps build support for our educational programs.

The ad hoc coalition in support of the tenants was not the first coalition or network we either helped form or joined. We know that tiny community programs such as ours cannot directly affect regional or national policy. There are an enormous number of similar programs, however, scattered throughout nearly every community in the country. Together we have the potential to raise a loud and persuasive voice on certain issues.

Several years ago, we joined other local youth-serving agencies to establish the West Side Task Force for Youth. Besides functioning as a referral and information-sharing vehicle for member programs, the Task Force is a forum for the discussion of policy matters and a powerful advocate for positions taken by member organizations.

At the level of citywide networking, we helped found Youth Engaged in Social Change. Originally a coalition of six change-oriented youth programs seeking to create a voice for young people in affecting policies concerning them, Y.E.S. Change has become an effective leadership-training program. Under the sponsorship of Advocates for Children of New York, youth participants have held their own speak-outs on educational and social issues and participated in various conferences, workshops, and media events to make sure the views of young people were adequately represented.

Recognizing the importance of access by young people to the media, The DOME Project in 1978 began trying to stir up some interest in starting a youth journalism project in New York City. The first year we spent contacting groups we thought might be interested in participating in or supporting such a venture. In the autumn of 1979, two journalism students from Columbia University volunteered to run journalism workshops for interested young people every Saturday at The DOME. The lack of a paper in which to publish workshop results contributed to the high turnover rate at these sessions, but eventually a group of seriously interested young people emerged.

Early in 1980 all the missing pieces seemed to materialize. During the spring and summer three preview issues of *New Youth Connections* appeared, and a daily summer workshop drew over thirty regular participants. During the 1980–81 school year, *New Youth Connections* appeared monthly with a circulation of 60,000 copies per issue. Two adult advisors work with a youth staff of teenage editors, journalists, photographers, and cartoonists, as well as with the youngsters who handle layout and circulation. Staff members range in age from twelve to nineteen. Some are excellent students and some are dropouts. Ethnically and racially they are as diverse as the population of the city itself.

Originally dependent upon The DOME Project for space and funds, Youth Communications New York Center now has its own offices and its own not-for-profit corporate status and tax exemption. It is part of a national network of youth communications centers with branches in Chicago, Los Angeles, Oakland, Washington, and Wilmington, Delaware. If the New York program can continue to grow and attract adequate funding, it may try to extend its training and youth communication functions to radio and television as well.

At the national level, our program belongs to the National Coalition of Alternative Community Schools. One year Tommy (my former student who had to act tough in order to survive) and I served on its board of directors. This organization is a lively coalition of independent thinkers and survivor organizations dedicated to humanist values and democratic process. Many of our youngsters have had the privilege of visiting some of the member schools through exchanges initiated by ASPEN, a clearinghouse for student exchanges sponsored by the Robert F. Kennedy Memorial, and our program has received a number of visitors in return.

None of this coalition-building and networking would make any sense, however, if our program were not providing an important local service. I left the Youth Center in 1972 partly because I found myself making claims about both the organiza-

tion for which I was working and the center I was running that
I knew would not stand up to close scrutiny. One reason I have
insisted on continuing to teach, despite my many administrative
and fund-raising responsibilities, is that I don't want to get so
far from youngsters that I once again create a program that
exists more in my mind than in reality.

The DOME Project's dual role as local program and advocate
for change on a regional or even national level seems to me an
appropriate reflection of how we have tried to remain responsive to the greatest and most pressing needs of our youngsters.
Existing institutions are not meeting those needs, and our program functions in many ways as an alternative research and
development center, trying to come up with new or revised
strategies for solving difficult and resistant problems. The
DOME Project is by no means unique in this respect. There are
many other interesting models being tried in communities all
over the country.

It is clear that many public school systems across the land are
in deep trouble. It should be equally clear that they cannot solve
all their problems alone. For some of these problems, at least,
community resources are at hand if they can only be yoked to
the public school system in some mutually acceptable manner,
one that does not destroy the autonomy and community base
that makes them so potentially valuable in the first place.

Replica DOME Projects proliferating all over the country
would not solve America's education problems. Our program
constitutes but one type of alternative, designed to meet the
needs of a specific group of youngsters, from among many such
alternatives that have proved effective. People interested in
emulating us should not look in this book or elsewhere for a
blueprint. What was appropriate for our students, given the
staff and resources available at a particular time, might not work
for other youngsters in other situations. What does seem to
make sense is to note those qualities of our program that have
contributed to success where other institutions have failed and

examine one's own community to see how local application would have to differ.

Sometimes people dismiss our success by complaining that we can only accomplish as much as we have because we are able to finagle so much support for our teachers. I agree, and furthermore I think that's a powerful compliment, not a criticism. We have ten salaried staff members and an important number of interns and volunteers teaching sixty-five youngsters. Most of our staff members, however, earn a modest, by New York City standards, $11,000 per year. Even figuring in the full cost of the Board of Education salaries and fringe benefits, our 1980–81 cost per pupil was still under $3000, as compared with the Board of Education's $8072 expenditure per pupil in 1979–80 for youngsters in special education programs. While the Board's figures include transportation costs and many other expenses not relevant to our program (we don't, for example, pay rent or utility costs at any of our sites, and we don't have physically handicapped youngsters requiring special equipment or attendants), it seems clear that our classes are still relatively inexpensive by comparison. In addition, the members of our instructional staff also run after-school and summer program components, participate in our community organizing activities, and perform many other important functions that multiply the value of each salary paid.

It is impossible to judge accurately the impact of a program such as ours on a community or even on an individual youngster. We do not monitor control groups that have the same problems as our youngsters but receive none of the same services. Perhaps those we feel we have helped would have done just as well or better without us. We like to think we have made a difference in the lives of many youngsters, however. Evidently some of them agree. Perhaps we have kept a few of the more seriously at risk from being separated from their families and either placed in custodial institutions or incarcerated.

The cost of our program certainly seems reasonable enough

when compared to the cost of full institutional care for young people. New York City's average per-child support to foster-care institutions in 1977 was already $24,000 per year. The cost of housing a youngster at New York City's Spofford Juvenile Detention Center is $187 per day, according to city estimates, a figure that translates into more than $65,000 per year per juvenile. We can run our entire program, including outreach and all other components, for less than what it costs annually to hold half a dozen youngsters in that overcrowded and de-grading facility.

I am not suggesting that our work keeps six young people out of jail every year or a dozen out of institutional foster care. We do work with hundreds of youngsters, however, many of whom are in trouble or on the fringes of it. We also work with many parents in an effort to help them cope with perhaps the most difficult period in their children's lives. It is certainly possible that we divert enough youngsters from various forms of institutional care through our preventive and supportive services to warrant a much more substantial budget and still argue that we would be saving society money.

Roughly 10 percent of the youngsters who comprise New York City's potential school enrollment are chronic truants, and nearly half of those who enter high school leave before earning a diploma. Truants and dropouts are three to five times more likely to be arrested for juvenile crime than their peers and suffer twice the unemployment rate of high school graduates between the ages of sixteen and twenty-four. A 1977 report by the Economic Development Council of New York City indicated that 63 percent of all youth crimes in New York City were committed during school hours. The annual cost of youth crime in the city for that year was estimated at $329 million.

I hate to argue for social programs on the basis of economics. What do dollar figures mean to a society that plans to spend $1.5 trillion for defense over the next six years while cutting back on subsidies for school lunches? What will there be left to defend in this country if we lose sight of the human cost of our economic decisions? Even if The DOME Project were substantially more expensive to run than it is, I would argue that its funding constitutes a better allocation of public money than pork-barrel dams and waterways, loans and subsidies for multinational corporations, and macabre missile systems.

I have derived enormous satisfaction from my work in the past eleven years. I have been privileged to work with many compassionate and dedicated people. The work itself has been challenging and worth trying to do well. We have created a program that has helped many young people cope with extremely serious and difficult problems. We have watched that program grow and prosper, and, somehow, we have managed to protect and sustain it without losing our willingness to take risks and commit ourselves to improbable tasks.

These successes, however, cannot obscure the failures and the memory of the many youngsters we could not help. The obstacles facing us and others engaged in similar struggles remain enormous. We may have helped a number of young people and touched other community residents in ways that have made their lives a little more pleasant or their prospects a little brighter, but we still live in a society that generates poverty and ignorance, violence and despair faster than we can hope to alleviate or reduce them.

The DOME Project is in its ninth year of operation, pretty decent longevity in a business in which new programs spring up and die out overnight. Each year we do a little more and do it a little better than the year before. Unfortunately, making it through one decade provides no guarantee we will make it through the next.

I still get my pink slip from the local school board every summer and undoubtedly will continue to do so until New York City gets its finances straightened out. One year the superintendent may not find a way to protect my job, and my career as a New York City public school teacher will end abruptly. If I falter in my yearly efforts to raise the dollar-for-dollar amount of private money needed to draw down public funds from the New York City Youth Board, Omar, Scott, George, and the rest of our core staff may have to look for other work. The VISTA allocations could be cut off from Washington at any time. But the problems won't go away, and neither will the youngsters. Someone will have to deal with them. Who will it be?

Chapter Fifteen

Working Against the Grain of Society

> *. . . everything was wanting that might give*
> *Courage to them who looked for good by light*
> *Of rational Experience, for the shoots*
> *And hopeful blossoms of a second Spring:*
> *Yet, in me, confidence was unimpaired . . .*
> WILLIAM WORDSWORTH
> *The Prelude*

I HAVE SPENT much of the past eleven years in a rage. I helped create The DOME Project, in part, as a vehicle for expressing that rage and turning it to constructive uses. Considering the alternatives, that choice was probably a wise one. I certainly risked becoming a very bitter person. Instead, every failure helped renew my determination, just as every sign of success buoyed my spirits and encouraged me to carry on.

Now, as I approach forty, my capacity for anger seems to be dwindling. I no longer find villains wherever I look in our society. Instead I see a welter of confused people caught up in a system they cannot control and only vaguely comprehend, a system that encourages them in so many ways to do as much as they can for themselves and as little for others as they can get away with.

I entered the 1970s ready to challenge "the establishment"

head-on, but like Br'er Rabbit trying to teach the Tar Baby a lesson, I found that the harder I'd swing, the deeper I'd get stuck, while the fox lay low in the bushes and chuckled. The campaign to shut down the welfare hotels convinced me that while direct political action has its place, I could make better use of my skills and energies trying to create alternative learning environments. Operating a community-based educational program within the public school system had its obvious limitations from the beginning, but it allowed me and my co-workers to develop what we felt were appropriate responses to the needs of our students while monitoring the effectiveness of public schooling for other youngsters. It gave us legitimacy as critics but also required us, as Luther Seabrook had challenged me early on, to put our money where our mouths were. Being alternative doesn't mean a thing if the alternative isn't better than the norm from which it sets itself apart; and being better, even when trying to provide an education for youngsters who seem to derive nothing but pain and frustration from their public school experience, has not always been easy.

Researchers now know enough about the human nervous system to recognize that individual children have different rates of growth and individual styles of learning. Most public schools, however, still require most youngsters to move at approximately the same rate through roughly similar programs. Even so diverse a school system as New York City's, with its special schools and vocational schools, its open classrooms and experimental classrooms, still offers few of its approximately one million students a sufficient range and number of choices. Most classroom teachers still talk, lecture, and demonstrate, while students sit, absorb, recall, and regurgitate. Education, for all the reforms and innovations of the twentieth century, remains largely as classroom-centered, teacher-controlled, and abstract as it was in the days when students did their homework by candlelight.

More than a decade ago, Neil Postman and Charles Weingartner, in *Teaching as a Subversive Activity*, summed up for me the dilemma posed by most schooling as it is still practiced in most school systems today. Although Postman subsequently repudiated their conclusions, I still find that many of their insights ring true. For example:

> It is not uncommon . . . to hear "teachers" make statements such as, "Oh, I taught them that, but they didn't learn it." There is no utterance made in the Teachers' Room more extraordinary than this. From our point of view, it is on the same level as a salesman's remarking, "I sold it to him, but he didn't buy it" — which is to say, it makes no sense. It seems to mean that "teaching" is what a "teacher" does, which, in turn, may or may not bear any relationship to what those being "taught" do.

Most urban schools seem more concerned with classroom management and maintaining pupil docility than in stimulating learning and creativity. Our classes at The DOME, on the other hand, all too often border on the chaotic. We do try to create some quiet periods as well, and we have to remember that some of our students don't concentrate very effectively when the classroom is full of distractions, but we try not to mistake passivity for attentiveness or docility for self-control.

It is not easy to determine what works best for any particular child. Often we must go through a prolonged and frustrating process of trial and error. Sometimes, after trying several different ways to get a point across, we will be surprised to hear a student respond, "Oh, is that what you mean? Why didn't you say so?" Of course, we thought we had been saying so all along; we just hadn't found the right way of communicating. Jean Houston, the noted humanist, once told me of a youngster who couldn't solve any of the math problems she gave him either orally or on paper, but when she tried tapping out the problems on his desk he was able to tap back the answers rapidly and accurately. He happened to be a gifted young drummer who was used to "thinking" with his fingers.

I am not suggesting that conventional modes of instruction are useless. They have helped millions of children and were once, in their own right, the revolutionary methods that helped transform education from the private province of those who could afford tutors or entered the service of the church into a mass activity designed to create a literate electorate and a working class able to cope with complex machinery. Most conventional classroom experiences, however, benefit primarily those students who can tolerate boredom, endure frustration, and defer immediate gratification for the prospect of increased future benefits. They also work best for those who have not been abused at home, deprived of a decent night's sleep, or sent to school on an empty stomach.

Most important of all, to benefit substantially from any extended and difficult activity, the participants must feel they have something worthwhile to gain from their involvement. If the benefits appear likely to outweigh the costs, most youngsters (like most adults) will participate in any process. They must believe in the potential benefits, however, and that is where our system, it seems to me, is in deep trouble.

For generations immigrant children have attended school in this country, firmly believing that an American education would provide the key to success. The more ambitious among them could hope to lose their accents, get good jobs, leave the ghetto where they were raised, and blend into the American mainstream. That version of the American dream, however, has resisted the most persistent attempts by black, brown, yellow, and red Americans to improve their lot through education. Racism has stood firmly in the way of all but a token minority. Nor has it helped that these groups have made their most dramatic efforts to advance just when America seems to have begun to run out of physical and economic frontiers promising unlimited expansion. When no one else has room to move up the ladder, the group on the bottom rung is also going to have to stay put. During the 1970s, New York City lost over 600,000 blue-collar jobs. Years ago high school dropouts could readily find factory employment; today even high school graduates often can't find any work at all. It was never a disgrace to leave school to take a job. Now many youngsters feel compelled to prolong school well beyond the point at which the experience may have any value for them simply because there are no jobs available if they leave. Entry into skilled and semiskilled trades and apprenticeships is likely to depend more on one's connections than on one's ability, and minority youngsters are unlikely to know anyone with clout. Ultimately any form of steady and respectable employment, let alone a shot at true upward mobility, remains for most nonwhite youngsters a matter of extremely intense competition for a severely limited number of openings.

As much as I disliked certain classes and teachers when I attended school, I understood it was in my interest to do my best. The youngsters I work with now, however, sense they have already been bypassed in the competition for attractive jobs by children with superior preparation and better connections. The alternative of working-class employment seems neither available nor particularly attractive, so youngsters find themselves hanging on in school with no sense of where more schooling will lead. Under the circumstances, it can only be expected to lead nowhere.

The real tragedy is that once society stopped needing these youngsters as workers, it ceased to have a place for them at all. Their primary function became providing employment for large numbers of teachers, welfare workers, corrections officers, and other public employees. In this respect they resemble garbage to be collected or sewage to be treated. Their numbers and distribution have some significance, but individual characteristics are meaningless.

Young people who realize that society has no positive role for them are likely to conclude they have nothing to lose by abandoning the difficult path of study and self-discipline for the instant gratification of street life. A few try to overcome the odds against them through excellence in sports or the performing arts. The promise of fame and riches can be as destructive as it is deceptive, however, and many a New York City playground is littered with the shriveling wine-drenched or drug-ravaged cadavers of would-be sports heroes who didn't make the big time and couldn't cope with the realization that their utility vanished with the spring in their legs and the quickness of their reflexes.

The only world open to every ghetto inhabitant who wishes to apply is the underworld. Every young prostitute gets her turn, and every mugger eventually finds a mark. These roles have their drawbacks, of course, but they are real functions available to anyone daring or desperate enough to try them. An enterprising teenage drug dealer may be able to turn over several hundred dollars in a few hours. The same youngster might have to expose an already fragile ego to rejection by dozens of employers and still be unable to find even a menial job netting him $20 for a hard day's work.

Because most of these youngsters venture only rarely from the far-flung ghetto areas buried conveniently out of sight and mind of the rich and the powerful, they remain invisible and neglected. From time to time, however, one emerges briefly into the harsh glare of the television klieg lights to titilate us with the horror of some violent act of mindless retribution. No matter that the anger in such youngsters is stirred by a society that promises them so much yet produces so little. When they finally do lash out, they invariably strike not some figure in a position of authority but an innocent individual who happens to be in the wrong spot when all that pent-up violence explodes.

In recent years America has increasingly relied on a law-and-order approach to dealing with this kind of street crime. I abhor violence as much as anyone, but I have little confidence we can contain or control it through the use of external force. I believe we would do better if we worried less about punishing wrongdoers after the fact and devoted more effort and resources to reducing the number of hopeless, depressed, and angry people in our society.

Rules are effective only so long as they are respected by enough people so that the violators can be isolated and dealt with effectively. When too many people begin to flaunt the rules there is something deeply wrong, and beefing up the police force or establishing mandatory prison sentences only begs the question. More than a strong police force and formidable penal system is needed. A peaceful and harmonious social system requires a shared sense among its citizens that its rules and institutions can function equitably for everyone. When that shared sense disappears, the police have as much chance of keeping a lid on crime as a substitute teacher does of maintaining order in a class in which all the pupils have decided to raise hell.

In one of the most stunning books I have read, *The Mountain People,* Colin Turnbull tells how members of a nomadic African tribe lose all vestiges of their traditional culture and subsequently all the social attributes we like to consider inherently human after they are forcibly transplanted from their customary foraging lands to an unfamiliar mountain preserve. Forced to adopt a totally unfamiliar way of life, the Ik, with whom Turnbull lived for two years, become totally selfish and devoid of consideration for one another. Turnbull tells of adults snatching partially chewed food from the mouths of dying elders or pushing children too old to nurse out of the home to starve to death on the doorstep. Turnbull concludes from his observations:

> If we grant, as the evidence indicates we should, that the Ik were not always as they are, and that they once possessed in full measure those values that we all hold to be basic to humanity, indispensable for both survival and sanity, then

221

what the Ik are telling us is that these qualities are not
inherent in humanity at all, they are not a necessary part of
human nature. Those values which we cherish so highly
and which some use to point to our infinite superiority over
other forms of animal life may indeed be basic to human
society, but not to humanity, and that means that the Ik
clearly show that society itself is not indispensable for
man's survival, that man is not the social animal he has
always thought himself to be, and that he is perfectly capable of associating for purposes of survival without being
social.

Reading *The Mountain People* reminded me of my students
who wrote about encountering the man who had no feet and
taking his shoes because he didn't need them. Deprived of an
environment sufficiently supportive to allow them to transcend
their own immediate needs and recognize and respect the needs
and humanity of others, these youths often respond to situations in very basic and frightening ways reminiscent of the Ik.

The DOME Project cannot make an imperfect social system
function effectively. We can, however, intervene in the lives of
a number of youngsters, creating a kind of growing space that
fosters a sense of belonging and personal worth during crucial
developmental years. When school personnel tell these young
people they are failures, when parents convey the message that
they are more a source of problems than pride, and when society seems to consign them to the scrap heap, we can help them
find ways to feel important without their having to exploit or
harm others.

One way to communicate to our youngsters how important
they are to us is to make ourselves available to them whenever
they need us, not just during school hours. Knowing we can be
reached at any time also gives them a sense of security and helps
overcome their feelings of alienation.

Another way we let youngsters know we care about them is
by kicking them in the behind when they need it. Young people
crave limits just as much as freedom. Despite their fussing

whenever the limits are enforced, they appreciate our efforts to draw clear lines wherever possible to help them understand which kinds of behavior are acceptable and which are not. One of our most difficult tasks, however, turns out to be finding ways of showing youngsters we can reject their behavior without rejecting them. Many young people have such fragile egos that criticism routinely sails right past the behavior it is intended to modify and threatens their sense of self-worth. One student invariably responded to even the gentlest criticism with some variation of "Why don't you love me anymore?" We often have to be careful to sandwich our critical comments between hugs just to make sure we are getting the right point across.

Several years ago I took four DOME students with me to a National Institute of Education workshop in Hot Springs, Virginia, in which the topic of discussion was "New Metaphors in Education." The opening session was devoted to a review of metaphors that were popular during various periods of our history to describe the educational experience (the empty vessel to be filled, the garden to be cultivated, the laboratory). Toward the end of the presentation, someone asked my students to add their own metaphors for the schools they had known. One put forward "jail," another said "jungle." When their interlocutor then asked them to describe The DOME Project, all four simultaneously blurted out "family."

I have since thought a great deal about that unrehearsed response, particularly as I have heard it recur frequently when our youngsters are asked to describe our program. Certainly it encompasses the sense of caring we have tried to build into our relationships. It also conveys a sense of close identification, something youngsters cannot often feel for the institutions in their lives. At its best, the concept of family implies a sense of mutual responsibility as well as mutual support, both qualities we strive to develop and nurture.

As in actual families, the way adults act and interact in our program sets the tone for the behavior of our youth. We can design and implement all kinds of complex program components and use the most sophisticated instructional techniques, but if the youngsters don't enjoy being around the staff members or the staff members don't get along with each other, the project will fail. Whether we're building a dome or studying fractions, everything we do has an irreducible base in personal relationships. The stronger we can make those relationships, the greater the involvement we can expect from our youthful participants.

Once youngsters care for us and respect our views, we can begin establishing higher expectations for their behavior and find ways to make those expectations stick. These youngsters will try not to disappoint us, but many of them will also trust us sufficiently to share with us some of their failures. Close relationships of this kind help create an effective learning environment and suggest at least a partial answer to why young people who could not function in a regular school setting find our mixture of constant caring, informality, and family-style interaction a viable alternative.

In the first DOME classes, we dealt almost exclusively with social and emotional problems while neglecting academic matters. Some of our students began to feel better about themselves and have some confidence in their potential. Unfortunately, when it came time for them to compete at the high school level they found themselves unprepared, and their carefully assembled positive attitudes came crashing about them like a house of cards.

Later we would swing too far in the other direction, concentrating on academic progress at the expense of our students' enormous emotional and social needs. We found ourselves becoming increasingly like the public schools to which we had posited ourselves as alternative and equally doomed to failure. Finding the proper balance among responses to the many urgent needs of our youngsters is probably our most difficult — and still unresolved — problem.

Our program cannot remain at the level of responding to the many pressing needs of our youngsters, however. If it does, we run the risk of encouraging them to become dependent on our help. If our primary goal is to assist them to become happy, productive, and independent adults, they must learn to take responsibility for their own education and development. First, though, they must learn to recognize the consequences of their acts, for others as well as for themselves, and this does not come easily to young people who have grown up in a world they have had good reason to view as capricious and beyond their ability to influence.

One reason so many youngsters appear to have such a difficult time dealing with the long-range consequences of their behavior is that they have no long-term perspective on their lives. Few of the young people with whom we work have thought much about the kinds of adults they would like to become. Some have wildly unrealistic dreams, which is the same in the end as having no idea of future at all. For every youngster in our program who chooses an attainable career and works to prepare for it, there are ten nonreaders who want to be doctors and twenty half-pints who fantasize about becoming the next basketball superstar.

Why do so many of these youngsters hold on to unrealistic dreams instead of working toward viable career objectives? In *Black Boy,* the story of his youth, Richard Wright explained: "My fantasies were a moral bulwark that enabled me to feel I was keeping my emotional integrity whole, a support that enabled my personality to limp through days under the threat of violence."

Too many of our youthful dreamers will experience the slow grinding to dust of their hopes by the harsh millstones of time and poverty. No child prefers a cesspool to a swimming pool, a sewer grate or doorway to a warm bed. A youngster needs healthy surroundings in which to grow to emotional, moral, and physical maturity. Good food is important, but so are a sense of belonging and a sense of future prospects, qualities many candidates for our program utterly lack. Amiri Baraka (then LeRoi Jones) reminded us in *Blues People:* "What is so often forgotten in any discussion of the Negro's 'place' in American society is the fact that it was only as a slave that he really had one."

Poor, nonwhite parents can give their children a sense of belonging in the home, but once those youngsters step out the door they must contend with racism and economic stratification. The school system, unfortunately, reflects these insidious characteristics of our society and shares responsibility for conveying to large numbers of youngsters the idea that they have no rightful place in American economic and social life.

Every youngster who feels he or she has no function or role in society is a potential time bomb. Recognizing this problem is not enough. We at The DOME Project are trying to do our share to correct it, but we realize we are struggling against the momentum of current national policy. Society is cranking out floundering and directionless children at too fast a rate for us to keep pace, even in our own neighborhood, and the deficient logic being used to dismantle those services with the potential for alleviating the problem is speeding us toward catastrophe.

What we are doing at The DOME Project works. Not with 100 percent efficiency but consistently enough to justify our determination to continue. We have no panaceas to offer. We know that many young people are growing up in conditions that leave them with serious emotional problems compounded by a lack of basic skills. The DOME Project didn't create those problems, nor can we erase them with good will and hard work. We need a commitment from our society to accommodate all its citizens, a commitment America flirted with making in the 1960s and then backed away from a few years later when the economy began to weaken.

The United States rose to greatness on its seemingly unlimited natural resources and its ability to convince every white child, whether native born or immigrant, that he or she could share in the greatness that wealth and power conveyed. Today our society is in trouble, threatened by dwindling resources and the widespread conviction among nonwhite youth that they will never share in the wealth and productivity of the society in which they live. This book may do little to alter the circumstances that convinced these young people that society considers them worthless, but it can at least give the lie to the notion that such youngsters are inherently lazy, stupid, violent, or otherwise inferior. On the contrary, one might argue that some of their most serious problems arise from being too bright and too ambitious to accept the passive and unproductive role society has allocated for them in the 1980s.

Working against the grain of society, I fear I am unlikely to live long enough to see the day when the efforts of The DOME Project and similar programs become central to the concerns of our nation. Fortunately the value of each and every child lies not in society's ability to recognize it but in the potential within each child. Meanwhile, I do what I can, curse my inadequacies, and rejoice wholeheartedly in every success story we help write.